Este Dictrio Devocional pertenece a:

_____

mi COPA ESTÁ rebosada

SALMO 23:5

Saved To Serve
Salvo para Servir
International Ministry

¡Bienvenidas, amiguitas!

Acércate y recibe la experiencia de cómo Él dirige tu vida. Descubrirás lo maravilloso que es Dios. Adorarás al Señor a medida que le conozcas.

¡Estamos muy felices de que estén aquí! ¡Hemos orado mucho por ustedes y el Señor nos ha escuchado! Este es un nuevo viaje con Dios y estamos muy emocionados de recorrerlo con ustedes. Nuestras oraciones han sido para que aprendan a deleitarse en la Palabra de Dios y se acerquen a Él cada día más.

No podemos esperar más, es tiempo. Planifica, ora y comienza a leer la Biblia. La vida cotidiana puede presentarse como un obstáculo en tu camino; pasarán cosas que te harán cuestionar a Dios. Llegará la hora de dormir y sentirás frustración. Es por ello que debes planificar tiempo con el Señor. Ora por encontrar estos momentos y comienza.

No estás sola en esta batalla. Todos luchamos contra las cosas que a veces interfieren cuando intentamos servir a Dios.

Acércate más a ÉL. Dios nos tiene cosas buenas reservadas para todos. Comparte con nosotros en Facebook cómo Dios ha usado este Devocional para bendecirte.

Luisette

Antes de comenzar a estudiar la Biblia,
puedes memorizar el siguiente pasaje del libro de Josué:

Josué 1:8

"Nunca se apartará de tu boca
este libro de la ley, sino que de día
y de noche meditarás en él,
para que guardes y hagas conforme
a todo lo que en él está escrito; porque
entonces harás prosperar tu camino,
y todo te saldrá bien."

Entonces... ¿Cómo lo hago?

Para leer la Biblia, haz un plan simple y apégate a él. Claro que podrías planificar para leer luego de limpiar la casa, guardar los juguetes, hacer la limpieza de primavera, poner flores frescas en la mesa y encender una vela aromática antes de leer. (Parece un buen plan, pero no es fácil lograrlo)

El Devocional explica como leer la Biblia de manera sencilla.

La lectura de la Biblia no tiene por qué ser difícil, piensa en un plan sencillo. Incluso la Biblia, en el Salmo 119:130, nos anima con las palabras: "La exposición de tus palabras alumbra; Hace entender a los simples".

La Biblia es para gente sencilla. No es necesario ser teólogos para entenderla. El Espíritu de Dios nos dará todo lo que necesitamos.

.

Algunas ideas Simples para ayudarte a pensar cómo planificar para leer la Biblia.

1. …Puedes levantarte 15 minutos antes y leer al menos un capítulo de la Biblia.
2. …Puedes instruirte leyendo la Biblia antes de ver la televisión (de hacer pastelitos, coser una almohada o jugar softball)
3. …Puedes utilizar tu teléfono o tableta para escuchar un capítulo de la Biblia todos los días. Intenta leer mientras escuchas si es posible. (Puedes escuchar libros enteros de la Biblia mientras conduces)
4. …Puedes leer tu Biblia antes o después de una comida.
5. …Puedes leer tu Biblia antes de acostarte por la noche.

¿Cuánto debo leer al día?

Muchas veces, la gente nos pregunta cuánto deben leer al día.

No hay reglas establecidas sobre cómo se debe leer la Biblia. Simplemente comienza y verás cómo el Espíritu Santo te ayudará a crecer.

Puedes comenzar desde donde estés. Evita desanimarte.

... Puedes leer un capítulo al día.

... Puedes tomarte un descanso a la mitad de un capítulo y leer el resto del capítulo luego.

... Puede leer hasta que encuentres algo que realmente llame tu atención y te haga decir ¡Oh! ¡Un momento! Entonces para y lo contemplas. Toma notas en el Devocional y planea cambiar tu vida para adaptarla de acuerdo a lo que has leído ese día.

Nuestras oraciones son para ti.

Un plan Simple para ti

Para este Devocional,
te sugiero leer un capítulo cada día.
La mayoría de los libros de la Biblia se
pueden leer en menos de un mes.
A continuación, encontrarás una lista de
libros y capítulos que puedes elegir e ir
marcándolos cada vez que
termines uno.

NUEVO TESTAMENTO

Libro	N° de Capitulos	Si, lo hice
Evangelio de Mateo	28	
Evangelio de Marcos	16	
Evangelio de Lucas	24	
Evangelio de juan	21	
Hechos de los Apóstoles	28	
Epístola a los romanos	16	
Primera epístola a los corintios	16	
Segunda epístola a los corintios	13	
Epístola a los galatas	6	
Epístola a los efesios	6	
Epístola a los filipenses	4	
Epístola a los colosenses	4	
Primera epístola a los tesalonicenses	5	
Segunda epístola a los tesalonicenses	3	
Primera epístola a Timoteo	6	
Segunda epístola a Timoteo	4	
Epístola a Tito	3	
Epístola a Filemón	1	
Epístola a los hebreos	13	
Epístola de Santiago	5	
Primera epístola de Pedro	5	
Segunda epístola de Pedro	3	
Primera epístola de Juan	5	
Segunda epístola de Juan	1	
Tercera epístola de Juan	1	
Epístola de Judas	1	
Apocalipsis	22	

ANTIGUO TESTAMENTO

Libro	N° de Capitulos		Libro	N° de Capitulos	Si, lo hice
Génesis	50		Eclesiastés	12	
Éxodo	40		Cantar de los Cantares	8	
Levítico	27		Isaías	66	
Números	36		Jeremías	52	
Deuteronomio	34		Lamentaciones	5	
Josué	24		Ezequiel	48	
Jueces	21		Daniel	12	
Ruth	4		Oseas	14	
1 Samuel	31		Joel	3	
2 Samuel	24		Amós	9	
1 Reyes	22		Abdías	1	
2 Reyes	25		Jonás	4	
1 Crónicas	29		Miqueas	7	
2 Crónicas	36		Nahúm	3	
Esdras	10		Hageo	3	
Nehemías	13		Zacarías	3	
Esther	10		Malaquías	2	
Job	42		Zacarías	14	
Salmos	150		Malaquías	4	
Proverbios	31				

Atributos de Dios

1. Dios es una persona	Alabado sea Dios. Él no es sólo una persona, sino también mi Abba padre. Mi Papá. Gen.1:26-27
2. Dios es Espíritu	Alabado sea Dios. Puedo adorar en Espíritu y en Verdad. Hoy puedo estar en la voluntad de Dios. Juan 1:18 Alabado sea Dios. Puedo adorar en Espíritu y en Verdad. Hoy puedo estar en la voluntad de Dios. Juan 1:18
3. Dios es inmutable	Alabado sea Dios, Dios no cambia. Él no puede ser más Santo, más misericordioso ni va a tener más gracia mañana. ¡Dios es inmutable! Salmo 102
4. Dios es eterno	Alabado sea Dios. Puedo alabar a Dios hoy y continuar hasta la eternidad. Él es el Dios eterno. Alabado sea Dios. Salmo 119; Salmo 89; Salmo 90
5. Dios lo sabe todo	Alabado sea Dios porque no necesito preocuparme por el futuro. El Dios que es TODO ÉL CONOCIMIENTO tiene mi futuro en Sus manos. Alabado sea Dios. Salmo 139:1-6
6. Dios está en todas partes	Alabado sea Dios… Dios es para nosotros… Dios está con nosotros… Dios está en nosotros, Alabado sea Dios. Salmo 139: 7-12

7. Dios es prudente	Alabado sea Dios, Él es un Dios sabio y quiere compartir esta sabiduría conmigo. Alabado sea Dios. Romanos 16:27
8. Dios es todopoderoso	Alabado sea Dios, aunque uniéramos todos los poderes del mundo, nucleares, solares, hidroeléctricos, magnéticos, satánicos, etc., no estaría a la altura de la omnipotencia de Dios. Salmo 33:6-9
9. Dios es soberano	Alabado sea Dios, nunca está fuera de control. 1 Crónicas. 29:11-14
10. Dios es Santo	Alabado sea Dios, no hay nadie santo como nuestro Dios. Isaías 43:15
11. Dios es honrado	Alabado sea Dios, nuestro Dios es justo. Podemos vivir por su voluntad ya que Él es un Dios justo para nosotros. Salmo 9:3-4
12. Dios es devoto	Alabado sea Dios, aunque yo sea infiel, Él permanece Verdadero, Alabado sea el Dios en el que me puedo enfocar en la fidelidad de Dios y ser salvado de la desesperación. Salmo 36:5
13. Dios es Amor	Alabado sea Dios, ¡su amor compró a la gente libre! Alabanza a Dios por su amor eterno. 1 Juan 4:7
14. Dios es misericordioso	Alabado sea Dios, siente mi miseria y me envía ayuda. 2 Cor. 1: 3
15. Dios es gentil	Alabado sea Dios, por gracia Él nos ha dado la salvación. 1 Pedro 5:10
16. Dios es Bueno	Alabado sea el Señor. Dios es bueno. Su voluntad para nosotros es ser siempre bueno. Alabado sea Dios me muestra la bondad de salvarme. Marcos 10:18

7 Pasos Devocional

Pasaje de La Biblia / y Fecha

-----/-----/------

Lo nuevo

¿Has encontrado algo en el pasaje de hoy que sea nuevo para ti?
Puede ser un nombre, un lugar, una situación o un versículo que no recuerdas haber leído antes.

El factor sorpresa

¿Qué fue lo más importante e impactante que leíste hoy?
Qué te hizo decir: "¡Realmente me ha sorprendido!"

La presencia de Jesús en el pasaje

¿Encuentras a Jesús en este pasaje? ¿Hay algo que te recuerde la vida de Jesús? ¿Algo en el versículo te hace pensar en las palabras de Jesús o en la forma en que vivió?

El carácter de Dios

¿Quién dice Dios que es? Identifica el carácter de Dios en este pasaje, piensa en la advertencia de Dios, en el amor de Dios y en los planes de Dios. Escribe las cualidades que Dios transmite en el pasaje, identifica los atributos que has descubierto en su carácter. Una buena manera de empezar tu frase, es usando palabras como: Dios es, Dios dice, Dios hace, Dios quiere o Dios puede.
Repasa tus respuestas anteriores.

El siguiente paso

Pregúntate: "¿Ahora qué?". Si lo que he leído es cierto, ¿cómo puedo aplicarlo? ¿Qué haría de forma diferente? ¿Qué tengo que cambiar?

El momento de la oración

Es hora de orar y pedirle a Dios que te ayude. Escribe tu oración a Dios basándote en lo que has aprendido del pasaje y de las preguntas de hoy.

¿Cómo funciona este devocional?

Ore y elija un libro de la Biblia para leer.
(Cualquiera está bien, todos forman parte de la Palabra de Dios).

Comience desde el primer capítulo

Lea uno (o más) capítulo(s) al día.

Profundice en su diario siguiendo los 7 pasos meticulosamente.

Oración.

Ejemplo
Devocional 7 pasos.

1. Pasaje de La Biblia y fecha

Ejemplo: Jeremías 1   01   /   01   /   2023

2. Lo nuevo

¿Has encontrado algo en el pasaje de hoy que sea nuevo para ti?
Puede ser un nombre, un lugar, una situación o un versículo que no recuerdas haber leído antes.

Ejemplo: En Jeremías 1: 5, nunca supe que Dios conocía a una persona antes de nacer. Es asombroso.

3. El factor sorpresa

¿Qué fue lo más importante e impactante que leíste hoy? Qué te hizo decir: "¡Realmente me ha sorprendido!"

Ejemplo: En Jeremías 1: 7, "Y me dijo Jehová: No digas: Soy un niño; porque a todo lo que te envíe irás tú, y dirás todo lo que te mande. No temas delante de ellos, porque contigo estoy para librarte, dice Jehová."
En primer lugar, no sabía que Jeremías era joven. El profeta Jeremías suena como alguien muy viejo. Pero, lo más sorprendente es que Dios le dijo que no importaba que fuese tan joven y que Él mismo le daría las palabras para hablar. ¡Me encanta!

4. La presencia de Jesús en el pasaje

¿Encuentras a Jesús en este pasaje? ¿Hay algo que te recuerde la vida de Jesús? ¿Algo en el versículo te hace pensar en las palabras de Jesús o en la forma en que vivió?

Ejemplo
En Jeremías 1:5 vemos que Dios aparto a Jeremías Antes de darle vida. Dios lo escogió antes de nacer. Dios lo aparto para un plan con las naciones. Igual que a Jesús.

5. El carácter de Dios

¿Quién dice Dios que es? Identifica el carácter de Dios en este pasaje, piensa en la advertencia de Dios, en el amor de Dios y en los planes de Dios. Escribe las cualidades que Dios transmite en el pasaje, identifica los atributos que has descubierto en su carácter. Una buena manera de empezar tu frase, es usando palabras como: Dios es, Dios dice, Dios hace, Dios quiere o Dios puede. Repasa tus respuestas anteriores.

Ejemplo:
Versículo 5: El Señor habla
Versículo 17: El Señor manda
Versículo 18: El Señor hace
Versículo 19: El Señor está con las personas
Versículo 19: El Señor entrega

6. El siguiente paso

Pregúntate: "¿Ahora qué?". Si lo que he leído es cierto, ¿cómo puedo aplicarlo? ¿Qué haría de forma diferente? ¿Qué tengo que cambiar?

Ejemplo:
Si todo esto es verdad, entonces significa que Dios me conoció ANTES de que yo naciera y que puede cambiarme y ayudarme a ser una persona que se comunica.
¡Me gusta esa idea!
Estaré más interesada a partir de ahora en aprender a hablar con la gente. Le pediré a Dios que me ayude a perder la sensación de miedo o timidez, para poder hablar delante de la gente sin sentir nervios.

7. El momento de la oración

Es hora de orar y pedirle a Dios que te ayude. Escribe tu oración a Dios basándote en lo que has aprendido del pasaje y de las preguntas de hoy.

Ejemplo: Hoy puse mis oraciones en poder acercarme a la directora del ministerio de las clases dominicales y decirle que quiero ser parte del equipo. También estoy orando por tener el valor de compartir a Cristo con mis compañeros de trabajo.

1. The Bible: Passage_____ and Date_____

_____/_____/_____

2. The New Thing

What is one new thing that stands out to you in today's passage?
It may be a verse you don't remember reading before.

3. The Wow Factor

What was the most important and impactful thing you read today? What made you say, "Wow! I'm blown away."

4. The Presence of Jesus in the Passage

What points to Jesus and His life in this passage? Does any verse remind you of something Jesus said or the way Jesus lived?

5. The Character of God

Who does God say that He is? Identify attributes from God's character in this passage. A good way to start, is to use words like: God is, God says, God does, God wants, or God can.
Review your previous answers.

6. The 'So What' or the Next Steps

Now, ask yourself, 'So what?' If what you read is true, how will you apply this? What will you do differently? What has to change?

7. Time to Pray

It is time to pray and ask God to help you. Write down your prayer to God based on what you are learning from today's passage and questions.

1. The Bible: Passage_____ and Date_____

_____/_____/_____

2. The New Thing

What is one new thing that stands out to you in today's passage?
It may be a verse you don't remember reading before.

3. The Wow Factor

What was the most important and impactful thing you read today? What made you say, "Wow! I'm blown away."

4. The Presence of Jesus in the Passage

What points to Jesus and His life in this passage? Does any verse remind you of something Jesus said or the way Jesus lived?

5. The Character of God

Who does God say that He is? Identify attributes from God's character in this passage. A good way to start, is to use words like: God is, God says, God does, God wants, or God can.
Review your previous answers.

6. The 'So What' or the Next Steps

Now, ask yourself, 'So what?' If what you read is true, how will you apply this? What will you do differently? What has to change?

7. Time to Pray

It is time to pray and ask God to help you. Write down your prayer to God based on what you are learning from today's passage and questions.

1. The Bible: Passage_____ and Date_____

_____/_____/_____

2. The New Thing

What is one new thing that stands out to you in today's passage?
It may be a verse you don't remember reading before.

3. The Wow Factor

What was the most important and impactful thing you read today? What made you say, "Wow! I'm blown away."

4. The Presence of Jesus in the Passage

What points to Jesus and His life in this passage? Does any verse remind you of something Jesus said or the way Jesus lived?

5. The Character of God

Who does God say that He is? Identify attributes from God's character in this passage. A good way to start, is to use words like: God is, God says, God does, God wants, or God can.
Review your previous answers.

6. The 'So What' or the Next Steps

Now, ask yourself, 'So what?' If what you read is true, how will you apply this? What will you do differently? What has to change?

7. Time to Pray

It is time to pray and ask God to help you. Write down your prayer to God based on what you are learning from today's passage and questions.

1. The Bible: Passage_____ and Date_____

_____/_____/_____

2. The New Thing

What is one new thing that stands out to you in today's passage?
It may be a verse you don't remember reading before.

3. The Wow Factor

What was the most important and impactful thing you read today? What made you say, "Wow! I'm blown away."

4. The Presence of Jesus in the Passage

What points to Jesus and His life in this passage? Does any verse remind you of something Jesus said or the way Jesus lived?

5. The Character of God

Who does God say that He is? Identify attributes from God's character in this passage. A good way to start, is to use words like: God is, God says, God does, God wants, or God can.
Review your previous answers.

6. The 'So What' or the Next Steps

Now, ask yourself, 'So what?' If what you read is true, how will you apply this? What will you do differently? What has to change?

7. Time to Pray

It is time to pray and ask God to help you. Write down your prayer to God based on what you are learning from today's passage and questions.

1. The Bible: Passage_____ and Date_____

_____/_____/_____

2. The New Thing

What is one new thing that stands out to you in today's passage?
It may be a verse you don't remember reading before.

3. The Wow Factor

What was the most important and impactful thing you read today? What made you say, "Wow! I'm blown away."

4. The Presence of Jesus in the Passage

What points to Jesus and His life in this passage? Does any verse remind you of something Jesus said or the way Jesus lived?

5. The Character of God

Who does God say that He is? Identify attributes from God's character in this passage. A good way to start, is to use words like: God is, God says, God does, God wants, or God can.
Review your previous answers.

6. The 'So What' or the Next Steps

Now, ask yourself, 'So what?' If what you read is true, how will you apply this? What will you do differently? What has to change?

7. Time to Pray

It is time to pray and ask God to help you. Write down your prayer to God based on what you are learning from today's passage and questions.

16 Toda la Escritura es inspirada por Dios y útil para enseñar, para reprender, para corregir y para instruir en la justicia, 17 a fin de que el siervo de Dios esté enteramente capacitado para toda buena obra.

2 Timoteo 3:16-17

Oraciones

1. The Bible: Passage_____ and Date_____

_____/_____/_____

2. The New Thing

What is one new thing that stands out to you in today's passage?
It may be a verse you don't remember reading before.

3. The Wow Factor

What was the most important and impactful thing you read today? What made you say, "Wow! I'm blown away."

4. The Presence of Jesus in the Passage

What points to Jesus and His life in this passage? Does any verse remind you of something Jesus said or the way Jesus lived?

5. The Character of God

Who does God say that He is? Identify attributes from God's character in this passage. A good way to start, is to use words like: God is, God says, God does, God wants, or God can.
Review your previous answers.

6. The 'So What' or the Next Steps

Now, ask yourself, 'So what?' If what you read is true, how will you apply this? What will you do differently? What has to change?

7. Time to Pray

It is time to pray and ask God to help you. Write down your prayer to God based on what you are learning from today's passage and questions.

1. The Bible: Passage_____ and Date_____

_____/_____/_____

2. The New Thing

What is one new thing that stands out to you in today's passage?
It may be a verse you don't remember reading before.

3. The Wow Factor

What was the most important and impactful thing you read today? What made you say, "Wow! I'm blown away."

4. The Presence of Jesus in the Passage

What points to Jesus and His life in this passage? Does any verse remind you of something Jesus said or the way Jesus lived?

5. The Character of God

Who does God say that He is? Identify attributes from God's character in this passage. A good way to start, is to use words like: God is, God says, God does, God wants, or God can.
Review your previous answers.

6. The 'So What' or the Next Steps

Now, ask yourself, 'So what?' If what you read is true, how will you apply this? What will you do differently? What has to change?

7. Time to Pray

It is time to pray and ask God to help you. Write down your prayer to God based on what you are learning from today's passage and questions.

1. The Bible: Passage_____ and Date_____

_____/_____/_____

2. The New Thing

What is one new thing that stands out to you in today's passage?
It may be a verse you don't remember reading before.

3. The Wow Factor

What was the most important and impactful thing you read today? What made you say, "Wow! I'm
blown away."

4. The Presence of Jesus in the Passage

What points to Jesus and His life in this passage? Does any verse remind you of something Jesus said
or the way Jesus lived?

5. The Character of God

Who does God say that He is? Identify attributes from God's character in this passage. A good way to start, is to use words like: God is, God says, God does, God wants, or God can.
Review your previous answers.

6. The 'So What' or the Next Steps

Now, ask yourself, 'So what?' If what you read is true, how will you apply this? What will you do differently? What has to change?

7. Time to Pray

It is time to pray and ask God to help you. Write down your prayer to God based on what you are learning from today's passage and questions.

Oración para fuerza espiritual.

14 Por esta razón me arrodillo delante del Padre, 15 de quien recibe nombre toda familia en el cielo y en la tierra. 16 Le pido que, por medio del Espíritu y con el poder que procede de sus gloriosas riquezas, los fortalezca a ustedes en lo íntimo de su ser, 17 para que por fe Cristo habite en sus corazones. Y pido que, arraigados y cimentados en amor, 18 puedan comprender, junto con todos los santos, cuán ancho y largo, alto y profundo es el amor de Cristo; 19 en fin, que conozcan ese amor que sobrepasa nuestro conocimiento, para que sean llenos de la plenitud de Dios.

Oración para justicia

¡Hazme justicia, oh Dios!

Defiende mi causa frente a esta nación impía;

líbrame de gente mentirosa y perversa.

² Tú eres mi Dios y mi fortaleza:

¿Por qué me has rechazado?

¿Por qué debo andar de luto

y oprimido por el enemigo?

³ Envía tu luz y tu verdad;

que ellas me guíen a tu monte santo,

que me lleven al lugar donde tú habitas.

⁴ Llegaré entonces al altar de Dios,

del Dios de mi alegría y mi deleite,

y allí, oh Dios, mi Dios,

te alabaré al son del arpa.

⁵ ¿Por qué voy a inquietarme?

¿Por qué me voy a angustiar?

En Dios pondré mi esperanza,

y todavía lo alabaré.

¡Él es mi Salvador y mi Dios!

1. The Bible: Passage_____ and Date_____

_____/_____/_____

2. The New Thing

What is one new thing that stands out to you in today's passage?
It may be a verse you don't remember reading before.

3. The Wow Factor

What was the most important and impactful thing you read today? What made you say, "Wow! I'm blown away."

4. The Presence of Jesus in the Passage

What points to Jesus and His life in this passage? Does any verse remind you of something Jesus said or the way Jesus lived?

5. The Character of God

Who does God say that He is? Identify attributes from God's character in this passage. A good way to start, is to use words like: God is, God says, God does, God wants, or God can.
Review your previous answers.

6. The 'So What' or the Next Steps

Now, ask yourself, 'So what?' If what you read is true, how will you apply this? What will you do differently? What has to change?

7. Time to Pray

It is time to pray and ask God to help you. Write down your prayer to God based on what you are learning from today's passage and questions.

1. The Bible: Passage_____ and Date_____

_____/_____/_____

2. The New Thing

What is one new thing that stands out to you in today's passage?
It may be a verse you don't remember reading before.

3. The Wow Factor

What was the most important and impactful thing you read today? What made you say, "Wow! I'm blown away."

4. The Presence of Jesus in the Passage

What points to Jesus and His life in this passage? Does any verse remind you of something Jesus said or the way Jesus lived?

5. The Character of God

Who does God say that He is? Identify attributes from God's character in this passage. A good way to start, is to use words like: God is, God says, God does, God wants, or God can.
Review your previous answers.

6. The 'So What' or the Next Steps

Now, ask yourself, 'So what?' If what you read is true, how will you apply this? What will you do differently? What has to change?

7. Time to Pray

It is time to pray and ask God to help you. Write down your prayer to God based on what you are learning from today's passage and questions.

Juan 15:9

PERMANEZCAN EN MI AMOR.

EN LA Mañana

CUANDO ME LEVANTO

dame

Jesus.

1. The Bible: Passage_____ and Date_____

_____/_____/_____

2. The New Thing

What is one new thing that stands out to you in today's passage?
It may be a verse you don't remember reading before.

3. The Wow Factor

What was the most important and impactful thing you read today? What made you say, "Wow! I'm blown away."

4. The Presence of Jesus in the Passage

What points to Jesus and His life in this passage? Does any verse remind you of something Jesus said or the way Jesus lived?

5. The Character of God

Who does God say that He is? Identify attributes from God's character in this passage. A good way to start, is to use words like: God is, God says, God does, God wants, or God can.
Review your previous answers.

6. The 'So What' or the Next Steps

Now, ask yourself, 'So what?' If what you read is true, how will you apply this? What will you do differently? What has to change?

7. Time to Pray

It is time to pray and ask God to help you. Write down your prayer to God based on what you are learning from today's passage and questions.

1. The Bible: Passage_____ and Date_____

_____/_____/_____

2. The New Thing

What is one new thing that stands out to you in today's passage?
It may be a verse you don't remember reading before.

3. The Wow Factor

What was the most important and impactful thing you read today? What made you say, "Wow! I'm blown away."

4. The Presence of Jesus in the Passage

What points to Jesus and His life in this passage? Does any verse remind you of something Jesus said or the way Jesus lived?

5. The Character of God

Who does God say that He is? Identify attributes from God's character in this passage. A good way to start, is to use words like: God is, God says, God does, God wants, or God can.
Review your previous answers.

6. The 'So What' or the Next Steps

Now, ask yourself, 'So what?' If what you read is true, how will you apply this? What will you do differently? What has to change?

7. Time to Pray

It is time to pray and ask God to help you. Write down your prayer to God based on what you are learning from today's passage and questions.

1. The Bible: Passage_____ and Date_____

_____/_____/_____

2. The New Thing

What is one new thing that stands out to you in today's passage?
It may be a verse you don't remember reading before.

3. The Wow Factor

What was the most important and impactful thing you read today? What made you say, "Wow! I'm blown away."

4. The Presence of Jesus in the Passage

What points to Jesus and His life in this passage? Does any verse remind you of something Jesus said or the way Jesus lived?

5. The Character of God

Who does God say that He is? Identify attributes from God's character in this passage. A good way to start, is to use words like: God is, God says, God does, God wants, or God can.
Review your previous answers.

6. The 'So What' or the Next Steps

Now, ask yourself, 'So what?' If what you read is true, how will you apply this? What will you do differently? What has to change?

7. Time to Pray

It is time to pray and ask God to help you. Write down your prayer to God based on what you are learning from today's passage and questions.

1. The Bible: Passage_____ and Date_____

_____/_____/_____

2. The New Thing

What is one new thing that stands out to you in today's passage?
It may be a verse you don't remember reading before.

3. The Wow Factor

What was the most important and impactful thing you read today? What made you say, "Wow! I'm blown away."

4. The Presence of Jesus in the Passage

What points to Jesus and His life in this passage? Does any verse remind you of something Jesus said or the way Jesus lived?

5. The Character of God

Who does God say that He is? Identify attributes from God's character in this passage. A good way to start, is to use words like: God is, God says, God does, God wants, or God can.
Review your previous answers.

6. The 'So What' or the Next Steps

Now, ask yourself, 'So what?' If what you read is true, how will you apply this? What will you do differently? What has to change?

7. Time to Pray

It is time to pray and ask God to help you. Write down your prayer to God based on what you are learning from today's passage and questions.

1. The Bible: Passage_____ and Date_____

_____/_____/_____

2. The New Thing

What is one new thing that stands out to you in today's passage?
It may be a verse you don't remember reading before.

3. The Wow Factor

What was the most important and impactful thing you read today? What made you say, "Wow! I'm blown away."

4. The Presence of Jesus in the Passage

What points to Jesus and His life in this passage? Does any verse remind you of something Jesus said or the way Jesus lived?

5. The Character of God

Who does God say that He is? Identify attributes from God's character in this passage. A good way to start, is to use words like: God is, God says, God does, God wants, or God can.
Review your previous answers.

6. The 'So What' or the Next Steps

Now, ask yourself, 'So what?' If what you read is true, how will you apply this? What will you do differently? What has to change?

7. Time to Pray

It is time to pray and ask God to help you. Write down your prayer to God based on what you are learning from today's passage and questions.

Oraciones

tus OJOS

Vieron mi

Salmo 139:16

Embrion

1. The Bible: Passage_____ and Date_____

_____/_____/_____

2. The New Thing

What is one new thing that stands out to you in today's passage?
It may be a verse you don't remember reading before.

3. The Wow Factor

What was the most important and impactful thing you read today? What made you say, "Wow! I'm blown away."

4. The Presence of Jesus in the Passage

What points to Jesus and His life in this passage? Does any verse remind you of something Jesus said or the way Jesus lived?

5. The Character of God

Who does God say that He is? Identify attributes from God's character in this passage. A good way to start, is to use words like: God is, God says, God does, God wants, or God can.
Review your previous answers.

6. The 'So What' or the Next Steps

Now, ask yourself, 'So what?' If what you read is true, how will you apply this? What will you do differently? What has to change?

7. Time to Pray

It is time to pray and ask God to help you. Write down your prayer to God based on what you are learning from today's passage and questions.

1. The Bible: Passage_____ and Date_____

_____/_____/_____

2. The New Thing

What is one new thing that stands out to you in today's passage?
It may be a verse you don't remember reading before.

3. The Wow Factor

What was the most important and impactful thing you read today? What made you say, "Wow! I'm blown away."

4. The Presence of Jesus in the Passage

What points to Jesus and His life in this passage? Does any verse remind you of something Jesus said or the way Jesus lived?

5. The Character of God

Who does God say that He is? Identify attributes from God's character in this passage. A good way to start, is to use words like: God is, God says, God does, God wants, or God can.
Review your previous answers.

6. The 'So What' or the Next Steps

Now, ask yourself, 'So what?' If what you read is true, how will you apply this? What will you do differently? What has to change?

7. Time to Pray

It is time to pray and ask God to help you. Write down your prayer to God based on what you are learning from today's passage and questions.

1. The Bible: Passage_____ and Date_____

_____/_____/_____

2. The New Thing

What is one new thing that stands out to you in today's passage?
It may be a verse you don't remember reading before.

3. The Wow Factor

What was the most important and impactful thing you read today? What made you say, "Wow! I'm blown away."

4. The Presence of Jesus in the Passage

What points to Jesus and His life in this passage? Does any verse remind you of something Jesus said or the way Jesus lived?

5. The Character of God

Who does God say that He is? Identify attributes from God's character in this passage. A good way to start, is to use words like: God is, God says, God does, God wants, or God can.
Review your previous answers.

6. The 'So What' or the Next Steps

Now, ask yourself, 'So what?' If what you read is true, how will you apply this? What will you do differently? What has to change?

7. Time to Pray

It is time to pray and ask God to help you. Write down your prayer to God based on what you are learning from today's passage and questions.

Oración de Jesús

17 Después de que Jesús dijo esto, dirigió la mirada al cielo y oró así: «Padre, ha llegado la hora. Glorifica a tu Hijo, para que tu Hijo te glorifique a ti, 2 ya que le has conferido autoridad sobre todo mortal para que él les conceda vida eterna a todos los que le has dado. 3 Y esta es la vida eterna: que te conozcan a ti, el único Dios verdadero, y a Jesucristo, a quien tú has enviado. 4 Yo te he glorificado en la tierra, y he llevado a cabo la obra que me encomendaste. 5 Y ahora, Padre, glorifícame en tu presencia con la gloria que tuve contigo antes de que el mundo existiera.

Jesús ora por todos los creyentes

20 »No ruego solo por estos. Ruego también por los que han de creer en mí por el mensaje de ellos, 21 para que todos sean uno. Padre, así como tú estás en mí y yo en ti, permite que ellos también estén en nosotros, para que el mundo crea que tú me has enviado. 22 Yo les he dado la gloria que me diste, para que sean uno, así como nosotros somos uno: 23 yo en ellos y tú en mí. Permite que alcancen la perfección en la unidad, y así el mundo reconozca que tú me enviaste y que los has amado a ellos tal como me has amado a mí. 24 »Padre, quiero que los que me has dado estén conmigo donde yo estoy. Que vean mi gloria, la gloria que me has dado porque me amaste desde antes de la creación del mundo. 25 »Padre justo, aunque el mundo no te conoce, yo sí te conozco, y estos reconocen que tú me enviaste. 26 Yo les he dado a conocer quién eres, y seguiré

haciéndolo, para que el amor con que me has amado esté en ellos, y yo mismo esté en ellos».

Jesús ora por sus discípulos

[6] »A los que me diste del mundo les he revelado quién eres. Eran tuyos; tú me los diste y ellos han obedecido tu palabra. [7] Ahora saben que todo lo que me has dado viene de ti, [8] porque les he entregado las palabras que me diste, y ellos las aceptaron; saben con certeza que salí de ti, y han creído que tú me enviaste. [9] Ruego por ellos. No ruego por el mundo, sino por los que me has dado, porque son tuyos. [10] Todo lo que yo tengo es tuyo, y todo lo que tú tienes es mío; y por medio de ellos he sido glorificado. [11] Ya no voy a estar por más tiempo en el mundo, pero ellos están todavía en el mundo, y yo vuelvo a ti.

»Padre santo, protégelos con el poder de tu nombre, el nombre que me diste, para que sean uno, lo mismo que nosotros. [12] Mientras estaba con ellos, los protegía y los preservaba mediante el nombre que me diste, y ninguno se perdió sino aquel que nació para perderse, a fin de que se cumpliera la Escritura. [13] »Ahora vuelvo a ti, pero digo estas cosas mientras todavía estoy en el mundo, para que tengan mi alegría en plenitud. [14] Yo les he entregado tu palabra, y el mundo los ha odiado porque no son del mundo, como tampoco yo soy del mundo. [15] No te pido que los quites del mundo, sino que los protejas del maligno. [16] Ellos no son del mundo, como tampoco lo soy yo. [17] Santifícalos en la verdad; tu palabra es la verdad. [18] Como tú me enviaste al mundo, yo los envío también al mundo. [19] Y por ellos me santifico a mí mismo, para que también ellos sean santificados en la verdad.

1. The Bible: Passage_____ and Date_____

_____/_____/_____

2. The New Thing

What is one new thing that stands out to you in today's passage?
It may be a verse you don't remember reading before.

3. The Wow Factor

What was the most important and impactful thing you read today? What made you say, "Wow! I'm blown away."

4. The Presence of Jesus in the Passage

What points to Jesus and His life in this passage? Does any verse remind you of something Jesus said or the way Jesus lived?

5. The Character of God

Who does God say that He is? Identify attributes from God's character in this passage. A good way to start, is to use words like: God is, God says, God does, God wants, or God can.
Review your previous answers.

6. The 'So What' or the Next Steps

Now, ask yourself, 'So what?' If what you read is true, how will you apply this? What will you do differently? What has to change?

7. Time to Pray

It is time to pray and ask God to help you. Write down your prayer to God based on what you are learning from today's passage and questions.

1. The Bible: Passage_____ and Date_____

_____/_____/_____

2. The New Thing

What is one new thing that stands out to you in today's passage?
It may be a verse you don't remember reading before.

3. The Wow Factor

What was the most important and impactful thing you read today? What made you say, "Wow! I'm blown away."

4. The Presence of Jesus in the Passage

What points to Jesus and His life in this passage? Does any verse remind you of something Jesus said or the way Jesus lived?

5. The Character of God

Who does God say that He is? Identify attributes from God's character in this passage. A good way to start, is to use words like: God is, God says, God does, God wants, or God can.
Review your previous answers.

6. The 'So What' or the Next Steps

Now, ask yourself, 'So what?' If what you read is true, how will you apply this? What will you do differently? What has to change?

7. Time to Pray

It is time to pray and ask God to help you. Write down your prayer to God based on what you are learning from today's passage and questions.

mi COPA

ESTÁ

rebOSADA

SALMO
23:5

Oraciones

1. The Bible: Passage_____ and Date_____

_____/_____/_____

2. The New Thing

What is one new thing that stands out to you in today's passage?
It may be a verse you don't remember reading before.

3. The Wow Factor

What was the most important and impactful thing you read today? What made you say, "Wow! I'm blown away."

4. The Presence of Jesus in the Passage

What points to Jesus and His life in this passage? Does any verse remind you of something Jesus said or the way Jesus lived?

5. The Character of God

Who does God say that He is? Identify attributes from God's character in this passage. A good way to start, is to use words like: God is, God says, God does, God wants, or God can.
Review your previous answers.

6. The 'So What' or the Next Steps

Now, ask yourself, 'So what?' If what you read is true, how will you apply this? What will you do differently? What has to change?

7. Time to Pray

It is time to pray and ask God to help you. Write down your prayer to God based on what you are learning from today's passage and questions.

1. The Bible: Passage_____ and Date_____

_____/_____/_____

2. The New Thing

What is one new thing that stands out to you in today's passage?
It may be a verse you don't remember reading before.

3. The Wow Factor

What was the most important and impactful thing you read today? What made you say, "Wow! I'm blown away."

4. The Presence of Jesus in the Passage

What points to Jesus and His life in this passage? Does any verse remind you of something Jesus said or the way Jesus lived?

5. The Character of God

Who does God say that He is? Identify attributes from God's character in this passage. A good way to start, is to use words like: God is, God says, God does, God wants, or God can.
Review your previous answers.

6. The 'So What' or the Next Steps

Now, ask yourself, 'So what?' If what you read is true, how will you apply this? What will you do differently? What has to change?

7. Time to Pray

It is time to pray and ask God to help you. Write down your prayer to God based on what you are learning from today's passage and questions.

1. The Bible: Passage_____ and Date_____

_____/_____/_____

2. The New Thing

What is one new thing that stands out to you in today's passage?
It may be a verse you don't remember reading before.

3. The Wow Factor

What was the most important and impactful thing you read today? What made you say, "Wow! I'm blown away."

4. The Presence of Jesus in the Passage

What points to Jesus and His life in this passage? Does any verse remind you of something Jesus said or the way Jesus lived?

5. The Character of God

Who does God say that He is? Identify attributes from God's character in this passage. A good way to start, is to use words like: God is, God says, God does, God wants, or God can.
Review your previous answers.

6. The 'So What' or the Next Steps

Now, ask yourself, 'So what?' If what you read is true, how will you apply this? What will you do differently? What has to change?

7. Time to Pray

It is time to pray and ask God to help you. Write down your prayer to God based on what you are learning from today's passage and questions.

1. The Bible: Passage_____ and Date_____

_____/_____/_____

2. The New Thing

What is one new thing that stands out to you in today's passage?
It may be a verse you don't remember reading before.

3. The Wow Factor

What was the most important and impactful thing you read today? What made you say, "Wow! I'm blown away."

4. The Presence of Jesus in the Passage

What points to Jesus and His life in this passage? Does any verse remind you of something Jesus said or the way Jesus lived?

5. The Character of God

Who does God say that He is? Identify attributes from God's character in this passage. A good way to start, is to use words like: God is, God says, God does, God wants, or God can.
Review your previous answers.

6. The 'So What' or the Next Steps

Now, ask yourself, 'So what?' If what you read is true, how will you apply this? What will you do differently? What has to change?

7. Time to Pray

It is time to pray and ask God to help you. Write down your prayer to God based on what you are learning from today's passage and questions.

1. The Bible: Passage_____ and Date_____

_____/_____/_____

2. The New Thing

What is one new thing that stands out to you in today's passage?
It may be a verse you don't remember reading before.

3. The Wow Factor

What was the most important and impactful thing you read today? What made you say, "Wow! I'm blown away."

4. The Presence of Jesus in the Passage

What points to Jesus and His life in this passage? Does any verse remind you of something Jesus said or the way Jesus lived?

5. The Character of God

Who does God say that He is? Identify attributes from God's character in this passage. A good way to start, is to use words like: God is, God says, God does, God wants, or God can.
Review your previous answers.

6. The 'So What' or the Next Steps

Now, ask yourself, 'So what?' If what you read is true, how will you apply this? What will you do differently? What has to change?

7. Time to Pray

It is time to pray and ask God to help you. Write down your prayer to God based on what you are learning from today's passage and questions.

Oraciones

⁵ Toda palabra de Dios
es digna de crédito;
Dios protege a los que
en él buscan refugio.

Proverbios 30:5

1. The Bible: Passage_____ and Date_____

_____/_____/_____

2. The New Thing

What is one new thing that stands out to you in today's passage?
It may be a verse you don't remember reading before.

3. The Wow Factor

What was the most important and impactful thing you read today? What made you say, "Wow! I'm blown away."

4. The Presence of Jesus in the Passage

What points to Jesus and His life in this passage? Does any verse remind you of something Jesus said or the way Jesus lived?

5. The Character of God

Who does God say that He is? Identify attributes from God's character in this passage. A good way to start, is to use words like: God is, God says, God does, God wants, or God can.
Review your previous answers.

6. The 'So What' or the Next Steps

Now, ask yourself, 'So what?' If what you read is true, how will you apply this? What will you do differently? What has to change?

7. Time to Pray

It is time to pray and ask God to help you. Write down your prayer to God based on what you are learning from today's passage and questions.

1. The Bible: Passage_____ and Date_____

_____/_____/_____

2. The New Thing

What is one new thing that stands out to you in today's passage?
It may be a verse you don't remember reading before.

3. The Wow Factor

What was the most important and impactful thing you read today? What made you say, "Wow! I'm blown away."

4. The Presence of Jesus in the Passage

What points to Jesus and His life in this passage? Does any verse remind you of something Jesus said or the way Jesus lived?

5. The Character of God

Who does God say that He is? Identify attributes from God's character in this passage. A good way to start, is to use words like: God is, God says, God does, God wants, or God can.
Review your previous answers.

6. The 'So What' or the Next Steps

Now, ask yourself, 'So what?' If what you read is true, how will you apply this? What will you do differently? What has to change?

7. Time to Pray

It is time to pray and ask God to help you. Write down your prayer to God based on what you are learning from today's passage and questions.

1. The Bible: Passage_____ and Date_____

_____/_____/_____

2. The New Thing

What is one new thing that stands out to you in today's passage?
It may be a verse you don't remember reading before.

3. The Wow Factor

What was the most important and impactful thing you read today? What made you say, "Wow! I'm blown away."

4. The Presence of Jesus in the Passage

What points to Jesus and His life in this passage? Does any verse remind you of something Jesus said or the way Jesus lived?

5. The Character of God

Who does God say that He is? Identify attributes from God's character in this passage. A good way to start, is to use words like: God is, God says, God does, God wants, or God can.
Review your previous answers.

6. The 'So What' or the Next Steps

Now, ask yourself, 'So what?' If what you read is true, how will you apply this? What will you do differently? What has to change?

7. Time to Pray

It is time to pray and ask God to help you. Write down your prayer to God based on what you are learning from today's passage and questions.

Oración de Ana

«Mi corazón se alegra en el SEÑOR;
en él radica mi poder.[a]
Puedo celebrar su salvación
y burlarme de mis enemigos.
2 »Nadie es santo como el SEÑOR;
no hay roca como nuestro Dios.
¡No hay nadie como él!
3 »Dejen de hablar con tanto orgullo y altivez;
¡no profieran palabras soberbias!
El SEÑOR es un Dios que todo lo sabe,
y él es quien juzga las acciones.
4 El arco de los poderosos se quiebra,
pero los débiles recobran las fuerzas.
5 Los que antes tenían comida de sobra
se venden por un pedazo de pan;
los que antes sufrían hambre
ahora viven saciados.

La estéril ha dado a luz siete veces,
pero la que tenía muchos hijos languidece.
⁶ »Del SEÑOR vienen la muerte y la vida;
él nos hace bajar al sepulcro,
pero también nos levanta.
⁷ El SEÑOR da la riqueza y la pobreza;
humilla, pero también enaltece.
⁸ Levanta del polvo al desvalido
y saca del basurero al pobre
para sentarlos en medio de príncipes
y darles un trono esplendoroso.
Del SEÑOR son los fundamentos de la tierra;
¡sobre ellos afianzó el mundo!
⁹ Él guiará los pasos de sus fieles,
pero los malvados se perderán entre las sombras.
¡Nadie triunfa por sus propias fuerzas!
¹⁰ El SEÑOR destrozará a sus enemigos;
desde el cielo lanzará truenos contra ellos.
El SEÑOR juzgará los confines de la tierra,
fortalecerá a su rey
y enaltecerá el poder de su ungido.

1. The Bible: Passage_____ and Date_____

_____/_____/_____

2. The New Thing

What is one new thing that stands out to you in today's passage?
It may be a verse you don't remember reading before.

3. The Wow Factor

What was the most important and impactful thing you read today? What made you say, "Wow! I'm blown away."

4. The Presence of Jesus in the Passage

What points to Jesus and His life in this passage? Does any verse remind you of something Jesus said or the way Jesus lived?

5. The Character of God

Who does God say that He is? Identify attributes from God's character in this passage. A good way to start, is to use words like: God is, God says, God does, God wants, or God can.
Review your previous answers.

6. The 'So What' or the Next Steps

Now, ask yourself, 'So what?' If what you read is true, how will you apply this? What will you do differently? What has to change?

7. Time to Pray

It is time to pray and ask God to help you. Write down your prayer to God based on what you are learning from today's passage and questions.

1. The Bible: Passage_____ and Date_____

_____/_____/_____

2. The New Thing

What is one new thing that stands out to you in today's passage?
It may be a verse you don't remember reading before.

3. The Wow Factor

What was the most important and impactful thing you read today? What made you say, "Wow! I'm blown away."

4. The Presence of Jesus in the Passage

What points to Jesus and His life in this passage? Does any verse remind you of something Jesus said or the way Jesus lived?

5. The Character of God

Who does God say that He is? Identify attributes from God's character in this passage. A good way to start, is to use words like: God is, God says, God does, God wants, or God can.
Review your previous answers.

6. The 'So What' or the Next Steps

Now, ask yourself, 'So what?' If what you read is true, how will you apply this? What will you do differently? What has to change?

7. Time to Pray

It is time to pray and ask God to help you. Write down your prayer to God based on what you are learning from today's passage and questions.

DE LA

Abundancia DEL

Lucas 6:45

Corazón

habla su boca.

La palabra
de Dios es
viva
y eficaz

Hebreo 4:12

1. The Bible: Passage_____ and Date_____

_____/_____/_____

2. The New Thing

What is one new thing that stands out to you in today's passage?
It may be a verse you don't remember reading before.

3. The Wow Factor

What was the most important and impactful thing you read today? What made you say, "Wow! I'm blown away."

4. The Presence of Jesus in the Passage

What points to Jesus and His life in this passage? Does any verse remind you of something Jesus said or the way Jesus lived?

5. The Character of God

Who does God say that He is? Identify attributes from God's character in this passage. A good way to start, is to use words like: God is, God says, God does, God wants, or God can.
Review your previous answers.

6. The 'So What' or the Next Steps

Now, ask yourself, 'So what?' If what you read is true, how will you apply this? What will you do differently? What has to change?

7. Time to Pray

It is time to pray and ask God to help you. Write down your prayer to God based on what you are learning from today's passage and questions.

1. The Bible: Passage_____ and Date_____

_____/_____/_____

2. The New Thing

What is one new thing that stands out to you in today's passage?
It may be a verse you don't remember reading before.

3. The Wow Factor

What was the most important and impactful thing you read today? What made you say, "Wow! I'm blown away."

4. The Presence of Jesus in the Passage

What points to Jesus and His life in this passage? Does any verse remind you of something Jesus said or the way Jesus lived?

5. The Character of God

Who does God say that He is? Identify attributes from God's character in this passage. A good way to start, is to use words like: God is, God says, God does, God wants, or God can.
Review your previous answers.

6. The 'So What' or the Next Steps

Now, ask yourself, 'So what?' If what you read is true, how will you apply this? What will you do differently? What has to change?

7. Time to Pray

It is time to pray and ask God to help you. Write down your prayer to God based on what you are learning from today's passage and questions.

Salmos 91

Oración para protección de Dios

¹ El que habita al abrigo del Altísimo

se acoge a la sombra del Todopoderoso.

² Yo le digo al SEÑOR: «Tú eres mi refugio,

mi fortaleza, el Dios en quien confío».

³ Solo él puede librarte de las trampas del cazador

y de mortíferas plagas,

⁴ pues te cubrirá con sus plumas

y bajo sus alas hallarás refugio.

¡Su verdad será tu escudo y tu baluarte!

⁵ No temerás el terror de la noche,

ni la flecha que vuela de día,

⁶ ni la peste que acecha en las sombras

ni la plaga que destruye a mediodía.

⁷ Podrán caer mil a tu izquierda,

y diez mil a tu derecha,

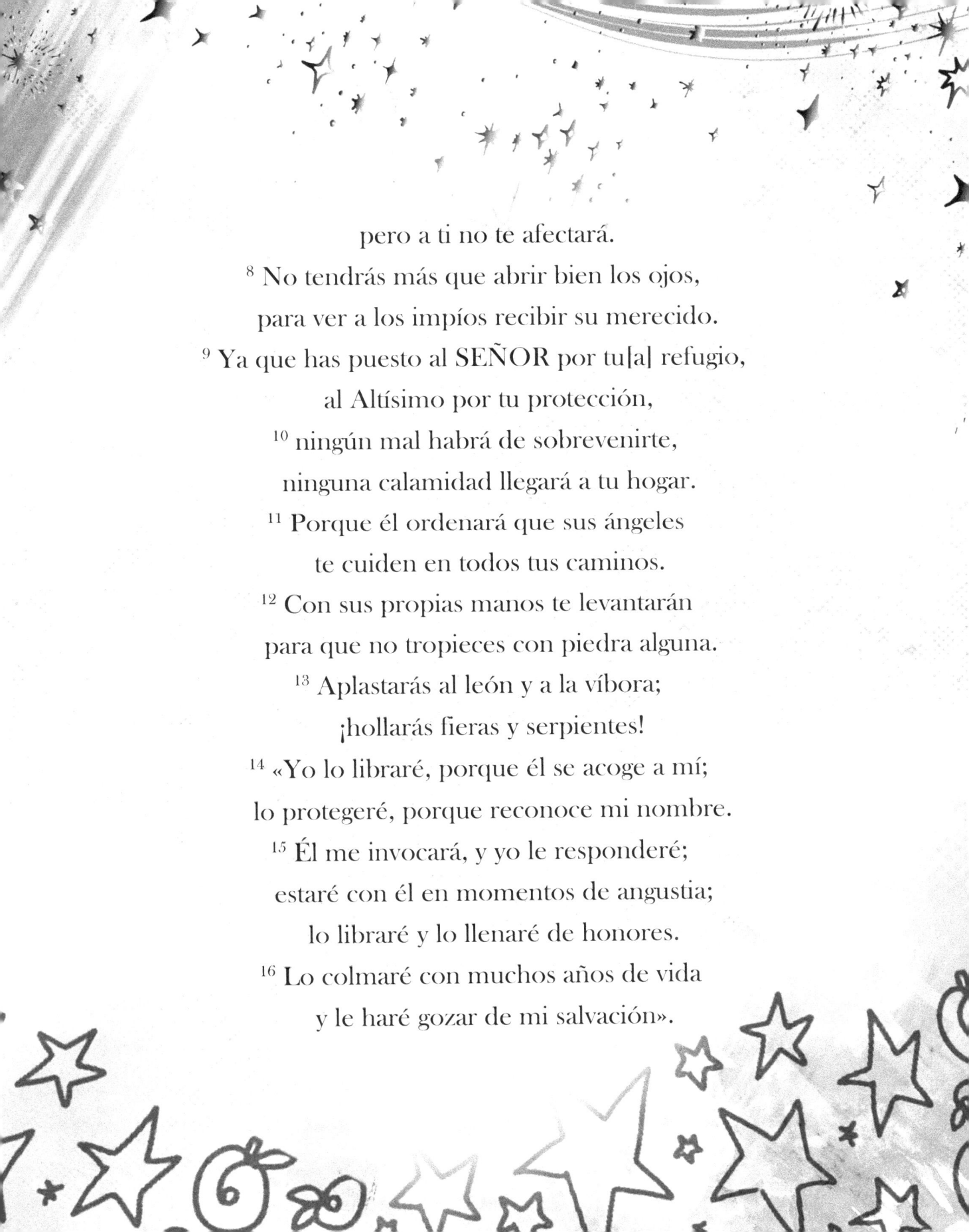

pero a ti no te afectará.

⁸ No tendrás más que abrir bien los ojos,
para ver a los impíos recibir su merecido.

⁹ Ya que has puesto al SEÑOR por tu[a] refugio,
al Altísimo por tu protección,

¹⁰ ningún mal habrá de sobrevenirte,
ninguna calamidad llegará a tu hogar.

¹¹ Porque él ordenará que sus ángeles
te cuiden en todos tus caminos.

¹² Con sus propias manos te levantarán
para que no tropieces con piedra alguna.

¹³ Aplastarás al león y a la víbora;
¡hollarás fieras y serpientes!

¹⁴ «Yo lo libraré, porque él se acoge a mí;
lo protegeré, porque reconoce mi nombre.

¹⁵ Él me invocará, y yo le responderé;
estaré con él en momentos de angustia;
lo libraré y lo llenaré de honores.

¹⁶ Lo colmaré con muchos años de vida
y le haré gozar de mi salvación».

1. The Bible: Passage_____ and Date_____

_____/_____/_____

2. The New Thing

What is one new thing that stands out to you in today's passage?
It may be a verse you don't remember reading before.

3. The Wow Factor

What was the most important and impactful thing you read today? What made you say, "Wow! I'm blown away."

4. The Presence of Jesus in the Passage

What points to Jesus and His life in this passage? Does any verse remind you of something Jesus said or the way Jesus lived?

5. The Character of God

Who does God say that He is? Identify attributes from God's character in this passage. A good way to start, is to use words like: God is, God says, God does, God wants, or God can.
Review your previous answers.

6. The 'So What' or the Next Steps

Now, ask yourself, 'So what?' If what you read is true, how will you apply this? What will you do differently? What has to change?

7. Time to Pray

It is time to pray and ask God to help you. Write down your prayer to God based on what you are learning from today's passage and questions.

1. The Bible: Passage_____ and Date_____

_____/_____/_____

2. The New Thing

What is one new thing that stands out to you in today's passage?
It may be a verse you don't remember reading before.

3. The Wow Factor

What was the most important and impactful thing you read today? What made you say, "Wow! I'm blown away."

4. The Presence of Jesus in the Passage

What points to Jesus and His life in this passage? Does any verse remind you of something Jesus said or the way Jesus lived?

5. The Character of God

Who does God say that He is? Identify attributes from God's character in this passage. A good way to start, is to use words like: God is, God says, God does, God wants, or God can.
Review your previous answers.

6. The 'So What' or the Next Steps

Now, ask yourself, 'So what?' If what you read is true, how will you apply this? What will you do differently? What has to change?

7. Time to Pray

It is time to pray and ask God to help you. Write down your prayer to God based on what you are learning from today's passage and questions.

1. The Bible: Passage_____ and Date_____

_____/_____/_____

2. The New Thing

What is one new thing that stands out to you in today's passage?
It may be a verse you don't remember reading before.

3. The Wow Factor

What was the most important and impactful thing you read today? What made you say, "Wow! I'm blown away."

4. The Presence of Jesus in the Passage

What points to Jesus and His life in this passage? Does any verse remind you of something Jesus said or the way Jesus lived?

5. The Character of God

Who does God say that He is? Identify attributes from God's character in this passage. A good way to start, is to use words like: God is, God says, God does, God wants, or God can.
Review your previous answers.

6. The 'So What' or the Next Steps

Now, ask yourself, 'So what?' If what you read is true, how will you apply this? What will you do differently? What has to change?

7. Time to Pray

It is time to pray and ask God to help you. Write down your prayer to God based on what you are learning from today's passage and questions.

⁴ Confío en Dios y alabo
su palabra;
confío en Dios y no
siento miedo.
¿Qué puede hacerme
un simple mortal?

Salmos 56:4

Oraciones

1. The Bible: Passage_____ and Date_____

_____/_____/_____

2. The New Thing

What is one new thing that stands out to you in today's passage?
It may be a verse you don't remember reading before.

3. The Wow Factor

What was the most important and impactful thing you read today? What made you say, "Wow! I'm blown away."

4. The Presence of Jesus in the Passage

What points to Jesus and His life in this passage? Does any verse remind you of something Jesus said or the way Jesus lived?

5. The Character of God

Who does God say that He is? Identify attributes from God's character in this passage. A good way to start, is to use words like: God is, God says, God does, God wants, or God can.
Review your previous answers.

6. The 'So What' or the Next Steps

Now, ask yourself, 'So what?' If what you read is true, how will you apply this? What will you do differently? What has to change?

7. Time to Pray

It is time to pray and ask God to help you. Write down your prayer to God based on what you are learning from today's passage and questions.

1. The Bible: Passage_____ and Date_____

_____/_____/_____

2. The New Thing

What is one new thing that stands out to you in today's passage?
It may be a verse you don't remember reading before.

3. The Wow Factor

What was the most important and impactful thing you read today? What made you say, "Wow! I'm
blown away."

4. The Presence of Jesus in the Passage

What points to Jesus and His life in this passage? Does any verse remind you of something Jesus said
or the way Jesus lived?

5. The Character of God

Who does God say that He is? Identify attributes from God's character in this passage. A good way to start, is to use words like: God is, God says, God does, God wants, or God can.
Review your previous answers.

6. The 'So What' or the Next Steps

Now, ask yourself, 'So what?' If what you read is true, how will you apply this? What will you do differently? What has to change?

7. Time to Pray

It is time to pray and ask God to help you. Write down your prayer to God based on what you are learning from today's passage and questions.

1. The Bible: Passage_____ and Date_____

_____/_____/_____

2. The New Thing

What is one new thing that stands out to you in today's passage?
It may be a verse you don't remember reading before.

3. The Wow Factor

What was the most important and impactful thing you read today? What made you say, "Wow! I'm blown away."

4. The Presence of Jesus in the Passage

What points to Jesus and His life in this passage? Does any verse remind you of something Jesus said or the way Jesus lived?

5. The Character of God

Who does God say that He is? Identify attributes from God's character in this passage. A good way to start, is to use words like: God is, God says, God does, God wants, or God can.
Review your previous answers.

6. The 'So What' or the Next Steps

Now, ask yourself, 'So what?' If what you read is true, how will you apply this? What will you do differently? What has to change?

7. Time to Pray

It is time to pray and ask God to help you. Write down your prayer to God based on what you are learning from today's passage and questions.

1. The Bible: Passage_____ and Date_____

_____/_____/_____

2. The New Thing

What is one new thing that stands out to you in today's passage?
It may be a verse you don't remember reading before.

3. The Wow Factor

What was the most important and impactful thing you read today? What made you say, "Wow! I'm
blown away."

4. The Presence of Jesus in the Passage

What points to Jesus and His life in this passage? Does any verse remind you of something Jesus said
or the way Jesus lived?

5. The Character of God

Who does God say that He is? Identify attributes from God's character in this passage. A good way to start, is to use words like: God is, God says, God does, God wants, or God can.
Review your previous answers.

6. The 'So What' or the Next Steps

Now, ask yourself, 'So what?' If what you read is true, how will you apply this? What will you do differently? What has to change?

7. Time to Pray

It is time to pray and ask God to help you. Write down your prayer to God based on what you are learning from today's passage and questions.

1. The Bible: Passage_____ and Date_____

_____/_____/_____

2. The New Thing

What is one new thing that stands out to you in today's passage?
It may be a verse you don't remember reading before.

3. The Wow Factor

What was the most important and impactful thing you read today? What made you say, "Wow! I'm
blown away."

4. The Presence of Jesus in the Passage

What points to Jesus and His life in this passage? Does any verse remind you of something Jesus said
or the way Jesus lived?

5. The Character of God

Who does God say that He is? Identify attributes from God's character in this passage. A good way to start, is to use words like: God is, God says, God does, God wants, or God can.
Review your previous answers.

6. The 'So What' or the Next Steps

Now, ask yourself, 'So what?' If what you read is true, how will you apply this? What will you do differently? What has to change?

7. Time to Pray

It is time to pray and ask God to help you. Write down your prayer to God based on what you are learning from today's passage and questions.

Oraciones

= TE BASTA CON MI =

Gracia

2 Corintios 12:9

1. The Bible: Passage_____ and Date_____

_____/_____/_____

2. The New Thing

What is one new thing that stands out to you in today's passage?
It may be a verse you don't remember reading before.

3. The Wow Factor

What was the most important and impactful thing you read today? What made you say, "Wow! I'm blown away."

4. The Presence of Jesus in the Passage

What points to Jesus and His life in this passage? Does any verse remind you of something Jesus said or the way Jesus lived?

5. The Character of God

Who does God say that He is? Identify attributes from God's character in this passage. A good way to start, is to use words like: God is, God says, God does, God wants, or God can.
Review your previous answers.

6. The 'So What' or the Next Steps

Now, ask yourself, 'So what?' If what you read is true, how will you apply this? What will you do differently? What has to change?

7. Time to Pray

It is time to pray and ask God to help you. Write down your prayer to God based on what you are learning from today's passage and questions.

1. The Bible: Passage_____ and Date_____

_____/_____/_____

2. The New Thing

What is one new thing that stands out to you in today's passage?
It may be a verse you don't remember reading before.

3. The Wow Factor

What was the most important and impactful thing you read today? What made you say, "Wow! I'm blown away."

4. The Presence of Jesus in the Passage

What points to Jesus and His life in this passage? Does any verse remind you of something Jesus said or the way Jesus lived?

5. The Character of God

Who does God say that He is? Identify attributes from God's character in this passage. A good way to start, is to use words like: God is, God says, God does, God wants, or God can.
Review your previous answers.

6. The 'So What' or the Next Steps

Now, ask yourself, 'So what?' If what you read is true, how will you apply this? What will you do differently? What has to change?

7. Time to Pray

It is time to pray and ask God to help you. Write down your prayer to God based on what you are learning from today's passage and questions.

1. The Bible: Passage_____ and Date_____

_____/_____/_____

2. The New Thing

What is one new thing that stands out to you in today's passage?
It may be a verse you don't remember reading before.

3. The Wow Factor

What was the most important and impactful thing you read today? What made you say, "Wow! I'm blown away."

4. The Presence of Jesus in the Passage

What points to Jesus and His life in this passage? Does any verse remind you of something Jesus said or the way Jesus lived?

5. The Character of God

Who does God say that He is? Identify attributes from God's character in this passage. A good way to start, is to use words like: God is, God says, God does, God wants, or God can.
Review your previous answers.

6. The 'So What' or the Next Steps

Now, ask yourself, 'So what?' If what you read is true, how will you apply this? What will you do differently? What has to change?

7. Time to Pray

It is time to pray and ask God to help you. Write down your prayer to God based on what you are learning from today's passage and questions.

1. The Bible: Passage_____ and Date_____

_____/_____/_____

2. The New Thing

What is one new thing that stands out to you in today's passage?
It may be a verse you don't remember reading before.

3. The Wow Factor

What was the most important and impactful thing you read today? What made you say, "Wow! I'm blown away."

4. The Presence of Jesus in the Passage

What points to Jesus and His life in this passage? Does any verse remind you of something Jesus said or the way Jesus lived?

5. The Character of God

Who does God say that He is? Identify attributes from God's character in this passage. A good way to start, is to use words like: God is, God says, God does, God wants, or God can.
Review your previous answers.

6. The 'So What' or the Next Steps

Now, ask yourself, 'So what?' If what you read is true, how will you apply this? What will you do differently? What has to change?

7. Time to Pray

It is time to pray and ask God to help you. Write down your prayer to God based on what you are learning from today's passage and questions.

1. The Bible: Passage_____ and Date_____

_____/_____/_____

2. The New Thing

What is one new thing that stands out to you in today's passage?
It may be a verse you don't remember reading before.

3. The Wow Factor

What was the most important and impactful thing you read today? What made you say, "Wow! I'm blown away."

4. The Presence of Jesus in the Passage

What points to Jesus and His life in this passage? Does any verse remind you of something Jesus said or the way Jesus lived?

5. The Character of God

Who does God say that He is? Identify attributes from God's character in this passage. A good way to start, is to use words like: God is, God says, God does, God wants, or God can.
Review your previous answers.

6. The 'So What' or the Next Steps

Now, ask yourself, 'So what?' If what you read is true, how will you apply this? What will you do differently? What has to change?

7. Time to Pray

It is time to pray and ask God to help you. Write down your prayer to God based on what you are learning from today's passage and questions.

Oraciones

130 La exposición de tus palabras nos da luz, y da entendimiento al sencillo.

Salmos 119:130

1. The Bible: Passage_____ and Date_____

_____/_____/_____

2. The New Thing

What is one new thing that stands out to you in today's passage?
It may be a verse you don't remember reading before.

3. The Wow Factor

What was the most important and impactful thing you read today? What made you say, "Wow! I'm blown away."

4. The Presence of Jesus in the Passage

What points to Jesus and His life in this passage? Does any verse remind you of something Jesus said or the way Jesus lived?

5. The Character of God

Who does God say that He is? Identify attributes from God's character in this passage. A good way to start, is to use words like: God is, God says, God does, God wants, or God can.
Review your previous answers.

6. The 'So What' or the Next Steps

Now, ask yourself, 'So what?' If what you read is true, how will you apply this? What will you do differently? What has to change?

7. Time to Pray

It is time to pray and ask God to help you. Write down your prayer to God based on what you are learning from today's passage and questions.

1. The Bible: Passage_____ and Date_____

_____/_____/_____

2. The New Thing

What is one new thing that stands out to you in today's passage?
It may be a verse you don't remember reading before.

3. The Wow Factor

What was the most important and impactful thing you read today? What made you say, "Wow! I'm blown away."

4. The Presence of Jesus in the Passage

What points to Jesus and His life in this passage? Does any verse remind you of something Jesus said or the way Jesus lived?

5. The Character of God

Who does God say that He is? Identify attributes from God's character in this passage. A good way to start, is to use words like: God is, God says, God does, God wants, or God can.
Review your previous answers.

6. The 'So What' or the Next Steps

Now, ask yourself, 'So what?' If what you read is true, how will you apply this? What will you do differently? What has to change?

7. Time to Pray

It is time to pray and ask God to help you. Write down your prayer to God based on what you are learning from today's passage and questions.

1. The Bible: Passage_____ and Date_____

_____/_____/_____

2. The New Thing

What is one new thing that stands out to you in today's passage?
It may be a verse you don't remember reading before.

3. The Wow Factor

What was the most important and impactful thing you read today? What made you say, "Wow! I'm blown away."

4. The Presence of Jesus in the Passage

What points to Jesus and His life in this passage? Does any verse remind you of something Jesus said or the way Jesus lived?

5. The Character of God

Who does God say that He is? Identify attributes from God's character in this passage. A good way to start, is to use words like: God is, God says, God does, God wants, or God can.
Review your previous answers.

6. The 'So What' or the Next Steps

Now, ask yourself, 'So what?' If what you read is true, how will you apply this? What will you do differently? What has to change?

7. Time to Pray

It is time to pray and ask God to help you. Write down your prayer to God based on what you are learning from today's passage and questions.

1. The Bible: Passage_____ and Date_____

_____/_____/_____

2. The New Thing

What is one new thing that stands out to you in today's passage?
It may be a verse you don't remember reading before.

3. The Wow Factor

What was the most important and impactful thing you read today? What made you say, "Wow! I'm blown away."

4. The Presence of Jesus in the Passage

What points to Jesus and His life in this passage? Does any verse remind you of something Jesus said or the way Jesus lived?

5. The Character of God

Who does God say that He is? Identify attributes from God's character in this passage. A good way to start, is to use words like: God is, God says, God does, God wants, or God can.
Review your previous answers.

6. The 'So What' or the Next Steps

Now, ask yourself, 'So what?' If what you read is true, how will you apply this? What will you do differently? What has to change?

7. Time to Pray

It is time to pray and ask God to help you. Write down your prayer to God based on what you are learning from today's passage and questions.

1. The Bible: Passage_____ and Date_____

_____/_____/_____

2. The New Thing

What is one new thing that stands out to you in today's passage?
It may be a verse you don't remember reading before.

3. The Wow Factor

What was the most important and impactful thing you read today? What made you say, "Wow! I'm blown away."

4. The Presence of Jesus in the Passage

What points to Jesus and His life in this passage? Does any verse remind you of something Jesus said or the way Jesus lived?

5. The Character of God

Who does God say that He is? Identify attributes from God's character in this passage. A good way to start, is to use words like: God is, God says, God does, God wants, or God can.
Review your previous answers.

6. The 'So What' or the Next Steps

Now, ask yourself, 'So what?' If what you read is true, how will you apply this? What will you do differently? What has to change?

7. Time to Pray

It is time to pray and ask God to help you. Write down your prayer to God based on what you are learning from today's passage and questions.

Hagan todo con Amor

1 Cor 16:14

Oraciones

1. The Bible: Passage_____ and Date_____

_____/_____/_____

2. The New Thing

What is one new thing that stands out to you in today's passage?
It may be a verse you don't remember reading before.

3. The Wow Factor

What was the most important and impactful thing you read today? What made you say, "Wow! I'm
blown away."

4. The Presence of Jesus in the Passage

What points to Jesus and His life in this passage? Does any verse remind you of something Jesus said
or the way Jesus lived?

5. The Character of God

Who does God say that He is? Identify attributes from God's character in this passage. A good way to start, is to use words like: God is, God says, God does, God wants, or God can.
Review your previous answers.

6. The 'So What' or the Next Steps

Now, ask yourself, 'So what?' If what you read is true, how will you apply this? What will you do differently? What has to change?

7. Time to Pray

It is time to pray and ask God to help you. Write down your prayer to God based on what you are learning from today's passage and questions.

1. The Bible: Passage_____ and Date_____

_____/_____/_____

2. The New Thing

What is one new thing that stands out to you in today's passage?
It may be a verse you don't remember reading before.

3. The Wow Factor

What was the most important and impactful thing you read today? What made you say, "Wow! I'm blown away."

4. The Presence of Jesus in the Passage

What points to Jesus and His life in this passage? Does any verse remind you of something Jesus said or the way Jesus lived?

5. The Character of God

Who does God say that He is? Identify attributes from God's character in this passage. A good way to start, is to use words like: God is, God says, God does, God wants, or God can.
Review your previous answers.

6. The 'So What' or the Next Steps

Now, ask yourself, 'So what?' If what you read is true, how will you apply this? What will you do differently? What has to change?

7. Time to Pray

It is time to pray and ask God to help you. Write down your prayer to God based on what you are learning from today's passage and questions.

1. The Bible: Passage_____ and Date_____

_____/_____/_____

2. The New Thing

What is one new thing that stands out to you in today's passage?
It may be a verse you don't remember reading before.

3. The Wow Factor

What was the most important and impactful thing you read today? What made you say, "Wow! I'm blown away."

4. The Presence of Jesus in the Passage

What points to Jesus and His life in this passage? Does any verse remind you of something Jesus said or the way Jesus lived?

5. The Character of God

Who does God say that He is? Identify attributes from God's character in this passage. A good way to start, is to use words like: God is, God says, God does, God wants, or God can.
Review your previous answers.

6. The 'So What' or the Next Steps

Now, ask yourself, 'So what?' If what you read is true, how will you apply this? What will you do differently? What has to change?

7. Time to Pray

It is time to pray and ask God to help you. Write down your prayer to God based on what you are learning from today's passage and questions.

1. The Bible: Passage_____ and Date_____

_____/_____/_____

2. The New Thing

What is one new thing that stands out to you in today's passage?
It may be a verse you don't remember reading before.

3. The Wow Factor

What was the most important and impactful thing you read today? What made you say, "Wow! I'm blown away."

4. The Presence of Jesus in the Passage

What points to Jesus and His life in this passage? Does any verse remind you of something Jesus said or the way Jesus lived?

5. The Character of God

Who does God say that He is? Identify attributes from God's character in this passage. A good way to start, is to use words like: God is, God says, God does, God wants, or God can.
Review your previous answers.

6. The 'So What' or the Next Steps

Now, ask yourself, 'So what?' If what you read is true, how will you apply this? What will you do differently? What has to change?

7. Time to Pray

It is time to pray and ask God to help you. Write down your prayer to God based on what you are learning from today's passage and questions.

1. The Bible: Passage_____ and Date_____

_____/_____/_____

2. The New Thing

What is one new thing that stands out to you in today's passage?
It may be a verse you don't remember reading before.

3. The Wow Factor

What was the most important and impactful thing you read today? What made you say, "Wow! I'm blown away."

4. The Presence of Jesus in the Passage

What points to Jesus and His life in this passage? Does any verse remind you of something Jesus said or the way Jesus lived?

5. The Character of God

Who does God say that He is? Identify attributes from God's character in this passage. A good way to start, is to use words like: God is, God says, God does, God wants, or God can.
Review your previous answers.

6. The 'So What' or the Next Steps

Now, ask yourself, 'So what?' If what you read is true, how will you apply this? What will you do differently? What has to change?

7. Time to Pray

It is time to pray and ask God to help you. Write down your prayer to God based on what you are learning from today's passage and questions.

⁹ ¿Cómo puede el joven
llevar una vida íntegra?
Viviendo conforme a
tu palabra.
¹⁰ Yo te busco con todo
el corazón;
no dejes que
me desvíe de tus
mandamientos.

Salmos 119:9-10

Oraciones

1. The Bible: Passage_____ and Date_____

_____/_____/_____

2. The New Thing

What is one new thing that stands out to you in today's passage?
It may be a verse you don't remember reading before.

3. The Wow Factor

What was the most important and impactful thing you read today? What made you say, "Wow! I'm blown away."

4. The Presence of Jesus in the Passage

What points to Jesus and His life in this passage? Does any verse remind you of something Jesus said or the way Jesus lived?

5. The Character of God

Who does God say that He is? Identify attributes from God's character in this passage. A good way to start, is to use words like: God is, God says, God does, God wants, or God can.
Review your previous answers.

6. The 'So What' or the Next Steps

Now, ask yourself, 'So what?' If what you read is true, how will you apply this? What will you do differently? What has to change?

7. Time to Pray

It is time to pray and ask God to help you. Write down your prayer to God based on what you are learning from today's passage and questions.

1. The Bible: Passage_____ and Date_____

_____/_____/_____

2. The New Thing

What is one new thing that stands out to you in today's passage?
It may be a verse you don't remember reading before.

3. The Wow Factor

What was the most important and impactful thing you read today? What made you say, "Wow! I'm blown away."

4. The Presence of Jesus in the Passage

What points to Jesus and His life in this passage? Does any verse remind you of something Jesus said or the way Jesus lived?

5. The Character of God

Who does God say that He is? Identify attributes from God's character in this passage. A good way to start, is to use words like: God is, God says, God does, God wants, or God can.
Review your previous answers.

6. The 'So What' or the Next Steps

Now, ask yourself, 'So what?' If what you read is true, how will you apply this? What will you do differently? What has to change?

7. Time to Pray

It is time to pray and ask God to help you. Write down your prayer to God based on what you are learning from today's passage and questions.

1. The Bible: Passage_____ and Date_____

_____/_____/_____

2. The New Thing

What is one new thing that stands out to you in today's passage?
It may be a verse you don't remember reading before.

3. The Wow Factor

What was the most important and impactful thing you read today? What made you say, "Wow! I'm blown away."

4. The Presence of Jesus in the Passage

What points to Jesus and His life in this passage? Does any verse remind you of something Jesus said or the way Jesus lived?

5. The Character of God

Who does God say that He is? Identify attributes from God's character in this passage. A good way to start, is to use words like: God is, God says, God does, God wants, or God can.
Review your previous answers.

6. The 'So What' or the Next Steps

Now, ask yourself, 'So what?' If what you read is true, how will you apply this? What will you do differently? What has to change?

7. Time to Pray

It is time to pray and ask God to help you. Write down your prayer to God based on what you are learning from today's passage and questions.

1. The Bible: Passage_____ and Date_____

_____/_____/_____

2. The New Thing

What is one new thing that stands out to you in today's passage?
It may be a verse you don't remember reading before.

3. The Wow Factor

What was the most important and impactful thing you read today? What made you say, "Wow! I'm blown away."

4. The Presence of Jesus in the Passage

What points to Jesus and His life in this passage? Does any verse remind you of something Jesus said or the way Jesus lived?

5. The Character of God

Who does God say that He is? Identify attributes from God's character in this passage. A good way to start, is to use words like: God is, God says, God does, God wants, or God can.
Review your previous answers.

6. The 'So What' or the Next Steps

Now, ask yourself, 'So what?' If what you read is true, how will you apply this? What will you do differently? What has to change?

7. Time to Pray

It is time to pray and ask God to help you. Write down your prayer to God based on what you are learning from today's passage and questions.

1. The Bible: Passage_____ and Date_____

_____/_____/_____

2. The New Thing

What is one new thing that stands out to you in today's passage?
It may be a verse you don't remember reading before.

3. The Wow Factor

What was the most important and impactful thing you read today? What made you say, "Wow! I'm blown away."

4. The Presence of Jesus in the Passage

What points to Jesus and His life in this passage? Does any verse remind you of something Jesus said or the way Jesus lived?

5. The Character of God

Who does God say that He is? Identify attributes from God's character in this passage. A good way to start, is to use words like: God is, God says, God does, God wants, or God can.
Review your previous answers.

6. The 'So What' or the Next Steps

Now, ask yourself, 'So what?' If what you read is true, how will you apply this? What will you do differently? What has to change?

7. Time to Pray

It is time to pray and ask God to help you. Write down your prayer to God based on what you are learning from today's passage and questions.

Oraciones

el

SEÑOR

te guiara

CONSTANTEMENTE

isaias 58:11

1. The Bible: Passage_____ and Date_____

_____/_____/_____

2. The New Thing

What is one new thing that stands out to you in today's passage?
It may be a verse you don't remember reading before.

3. The Wow Factor

What was the most important and impactful thing you read today? What made you say, "Wow! I'm blown away."

4. The Presence of Jesus in the Passage

What points to Jesus and His life in this passage? Does any verse remind you of something Jesus said or the way Jesus lived?

5. The Character of God

Who does God say that He is? Identify attributes from God's character in this passage. A good way to start, is to use words like: God is, God says, God does, God wants, or God can.
Review your previous answers.

6. The 'So What' or the Next Steps

Now, ask yourself, 'So what?' If what you read is true, how will you apply this? What will you do differently? What has to change?

7. Time to Pray

It is time to pray and ask God to help you. Write down your prayer to God based on what you are learning from today's passage and questions.

1. The Bible: Passage_____ and Date_____

_____/_____/_____

2. The New Thing

What is one new thing that stands out to you in today's passage?
It may be a verse you don't remember reading before.

3. The Wow Factor

What was the most important and impactful thing you read today? What made you say, "Wow! I'm blown away."

4. The Presence of Jesus in the Passage

What points to Jesus and His life in this passage? Does any verse remind you of something Jesus said or the way Jesus lived?

5. The Character of God

Who does God say that He is? Identify attributes from God's character in this passage. A good way to start, is to use words like: God is, God says, God does, God wants, or God can.
Review your previous answers.

6. The 'So What' or the Next Steps

Now, ask yourself, 'So what?' If what you read is true, how will you apply this? What will you do differently? What has to change?

7. Time to Pray

It is time to pray and ask God to help you. Write down your prayer to God based on what you are learning from today's passage and questions.

1. The Bible: Passage_____ and Date_____

_____/_____/_____

2. The New Thing

What is one new thing that stands out to you in today's passage?
It may be a verse you don't remember reading before.

3. The Wow Factor

What was the most important and impactful thing you read today? What made you say, "Wow! I'm blown away."

4. The Presence of Jesus in the Passage

What points to Jesus and His life in this passage? Does any verse remind you of something Jesus said or the way Jesus lived?

5. The Character of God

Who does God say that He is? Identify attributes from God's character in this passage. A good way to start, is to use words like: God is, God says, God does, God wants, or God can.
Review your previous answers.

6. The 'So What' or the Next Steps

Now, ask yourself, 'So what?' If what you read is true, how will you apply this? What will you do differently? What has to change?

7. Time to Pray

It is time to pray and ask God to help you. Write down your prayer to God based on what you are learning from today's passage and questions.

Oración de ayudo contra enemigos

Ten compasión de mí, oh Dios;
ten compasión de mí, que en ti confío.
A la sombra de tus alas me refugiaré,
hasta que haya pasado el peligro.
2 Clamo al Dios Altísimo,
al Dios que me brinda su apoyo.
3 Desde el cielo me tiende la mano y me salva;
reprende a mis perseguidores. Selah
¡Dios me envía su amor y su verdad!
4 Me encuentro en medio de leones,
rodeado de gente rapaz.
Sus dientes son lanzas y flechas;
su lengua, una espada afilada.
5 Pero tú, oh Dios, estás sobre los cielos,
¡tu gloria cubre toda la tierra!

⁶ Tendieron una red en mi camino,

y mi ánimo quedó por los suelos.

En mi senda cavaron una fosa,

pero ellos mismos cayeron en ella. Selah

⁷ Firme está, oh Dios, mi corazón;

firme está mi corazón.

Voy a cantarte salmos.

⁸ ¡Despierta, alma mía!

¡Despierten, arpa y lira!

¡Haré despertar al nuevo día!

⁹ Te alabaré, Señor, entre los pueblos,

te cantaré salmos entre las naciones.

¹⁰ Pues tu amor es tan grande que llega a los cielos;

¡tu verdad llega hasta el firmamento!

¹¹ ¡Tú, oh Dios, estás sobre los cielos;

tu gloria cubre toda la tierra!

1. The Bible: Passage_____ and Date_____

_____/_____/_____

2. The New Thing

What is one new thing that stands out to you in today's passage?
It may be a verse you don't remember reading before.

3. The Wow Factor

What was the most important and impactful thing you read today? What made you say, "Wow! I'm blown away."

4. The Presence of Jesus in the Passage

What points to Jesus and His life in this passage? Does any verse remind you of something Jesus said or the way Jesus lived?

5. The Character of God

Who does God say that He is? Identify attributes from God's character in this passage. A good way to start, is to use words like: God is, God says, God does, God wants, or God can.
Review your previous answers.

6. The 'So What' or the Next Steps

Now, ask yourself, 'So what?' If what you read is true, how will you apply this? What will you do differently? What has to change?

7. Time to Pray

It is time to pray and ask God to help you. Write down your prayer to God based on what you are learning from today's passage and questions.

1. The Bible: Passage_____ and Date_____

_____/_____/_____

2. The New Thing

What is one new thing that stands out to you in today's passage?
It may be a verse you don't remember reading before.

3. The Wow Factor

What was the most important and impactful thing you read today? What made you say, "Wow! I'm blown away."

4. The Presence of Jesus in the Passage

What points to Jesus and His life in this passage? Does any verse remind you of something Jesus said or the way Jesus lived?

5. The Character of God

Who does God say that He is? Identify attributes from God's character in this passage. A good way to start, is to use words like: God is, God says, God does, God wants, or God can.
Review your previous answers.

6. The 'So What' or the Next Steps

Now, ask yourself, 'So what?' If what you read is true, how will you apply this? What will you do differently? What has to change?

7. Time to Pray

It is time to pray and ask God to help you. Write down your prayer to God based on what you are learning from today's passage and questions.

Oraciones

¹¹ **En mi corazón atesoro tus dichos para no pecar contra ti.**

Salmos 119:11

1. The Bible: Passage_____ and Date_____

_____/_____/_____

2. The New Thing

What is one new thing that stands out to you in today's passage?
It may be a verse you don't remember reading before.

3. The Wow Factor

What was the most important and impactful thing you read today? What made you say, "Wow! I'm blown away."

4. The Presence of Jesus in the Passage

What points to Jesus and His life in this passage? Does any verse remind you of something Jesus said or the way Jesus lived?

5. The Character of God

Who does God say that He is? Identify attributes from God's character in this passage. A good way to start, is to use words like: God is, God says, God does, God wants, or God can.
Review your previous answers.

6. The 'So What' or the Next Steps

Now, ask yourself, 'So what?' If what you read is true, how will you apply this? What will you do differently? What has to change?

7. Time to Pray

It is time to pray and ask God to help you. Write down your prayer to God based on what you are learning from today's passage and questions.

1. The Bible: Passage_____ and Date_____

_____/_____/_____

2. The New Thing

What is one new thing that stands out to you in today's passage?
It may be a verse you don't remember reading before.

3. The Wow Factor

What was the most important and impactful thing you read today? What made you say, "Wow! I'm blown away."

4. The Presence of Jesus in the Passage

What points to Jesus and His life in this passage? Does any verse remind you of something Jesus said or the way Jesus lived?

5. The Character of God

Who does God say that He is? Identify attributes from God's character in this passage. A good way to start, is to use words like: God is, God says, God does, God wants, or God can.
Review your previous answers.

6. The 'So What' or the Next Steps

Now, ask yourself, 'So what?' If what you read is true, how will you apply this? What will you do differently? What has to change?

7. Time to Pray

It is time to pray and ask God to help you. Write down your prayer to God based on what you are learning from today's passage and questions.

1. The Bible: Passage_____ and Date_____

_____/_____/_____

2. The New Thing

What is one new thing that stands out to you in today's passage?
It may be a verse you don't remember reading before.

3. The Wow Factor

What was the most important and impactful thing you read today? What made you say, "Wow! I'm blown away."

4. The Presence of Jesus in the Passage

What points to Jesus and His life in this passage? Does any verse remind you of something Jesus said or the way Jesus lived?

5. The Character of God

Who does God say that He is? Identify attributes from God's character in this passage. A good way to start, is to use words like: God is, God says, God does, God wants, or God can.
Review your previous answers.

6. The 'So What' or the Next Steps

Now, ask yourself, 'So what?' If what you read is true, how will you apply this? What will you do differently? What has to change?

7. Time to Pray

It is time to pray and ask God to help you. Write down your prayer to God based on what you are learning from today's passage and questions.

1. The Bible: Passage_____ and Date_____

_____/_____/_____

2. The New Thing

What is one new thing that stands out to you in today's passage?
It may be a verse you don't remember reading before.

3. The Wow Factor

What was the most important and impactful thing you read today? What made you say, "Wow! I'm blown away."

4. The Presence of Jesus in the Passage

What points to Jesus and His life in this passage? Does any verse remind you of something Jesus said or the way Jesus lived?

5. The Character of God

Who does God say that He is? Identify attributes from God's character in this passage. A good way to start, is to use words like: God is, God says, God does, God wants, or God can.
Review your previous answers.

6. The 'So What' or the Next Steps

Now, ask yourself, 'So what?' If what you read is true, how will you apply this? What will you do differently? What has to change?

7. Time to Pray

It is time to pray and ask God to help you. Write down your prayer to God based on what you are learning from today's passage and questions.

1. The Bible: Passage_____ and Date_____

_____/_____/_____

2. The New Thing

What is one new thing that stands out to you in today's passage?
It may be a verse you don't remember reading before.

3. The Wow Factor

What was the most important and impactful thing you read today? What made you say, "Wow! I'm blown away."

4. The Presence of Jesus in the Passage

What points to Jesus and His life in this passage? Does any verse remind you of something Jesus said or the way Jesus lived?

5. The Character of God

Who does God say that He is? Identify attributes from God's character in this passage. A good way to start, is to use words like: God is, God says, God does, God wants, or God can.
Review your previous answers.

6. The 'So What' or the Next Steps

Now, ask yourself, 'So what?' If what you read is true, how will you apply this? What will you do differently? What has to change?

7. Time to Pray

It is time to pray and ask God to help you. Write down your prayer to God based on what you are learning from today's passage and questions.

Oraciones

1. The Bible: Passage_____ and Date_____

_____/_____/_____

2. The New Thing

What is one new thing that stands out to you in today's passage?
It may be a verse you don't remember reading before.

3. The Wow Factor

What was the most important and impactful thing you read today? What made you say, "Wow! I'm blown away."

4. The Presence of Jesus in the Passage

What points to Jesus and His life in this passage? Does any verse remind you of something Jesus said or the way Jesus lived?

5. The Character of God

Who does God say that He is? Identify attributes from God's character in this passage. A good way to start, is to use words like: God is, God says, God does, God wants, or God can.
Review your previous answers.

6. The 'So What' or the Next Steps

Now, ask yourself, 'So what?' If what you read is true, how will you apply this? What will you do differently? What has to change?

7. Time to Pray

It is time to pray and ask God to help you. Write down your prayer to God based on what you are learning from today's passage and questions.

1. The Bible: Passage_____ and Date_____

_____/_____/_____

2. The New Thing

What is one new thing that stands out to you in today's passage?
It may be a verse you don't remember reading before.

3. The Wow Factor

What was the most important and impactful thing you read today? What made you say, "Wow! I'm
blown away."

4. The Presence of Jesus in the Passage

What points to Jesus and His life in this passage? Does any verse remind you of something Jesus said
or the way Jesus lived?

5. The Character of God

Who does God say that He is? Identify attributes from God's character in this passage. A good way to start, is to use words like: God is, God says, God does, God wants, or God can.
Review your previous answers.

6. The 'So What' or the Next Steps

Now, ask yourself, 'So what?' If what you read is true, how will you apply this? What will you do differently? What has to change?

7. Time to Pray

It is time to pray and ask God to help you. Write down your prayer to God based on what you are learning from today's passage and questions.

1. The Bible: Passage_____ and Date_____

_____/_____/_____

2. The New Thing

What is one new thing that stands out to you in today's passage?
It may be a verse you don't remember reading before.

3. The Wow Factor

What was the most important and impactful thing you read today? What made you say, "Wow! I'm blown away."

4. The Presence of Jesus in the Passage

What points to Jesus and His life in this passage? Does any verse remind you of something Jesus said or the way Jesus lived?

5. The Character of God

Who does God say that He is? Identify attributes from God's character in this passage. A good way to start, is to use words like: God is, God says, God does, God wants, or God can.
Review your previous answers.

6. The 'So What' or the Next Steps

Now, ask yourself, 'So what?' If what you read is true, how will you apply this? What will you do differently? What has to change?

7. Time to Pray

It is time to pray and ask God to help you. Write down your prayer to God based on what you are learning from today's passage and questions.

1. The Bible: Passage_____ and Date_____

_____/_____/_____

2. The New Thing

What is one new thing that stands out to you in today's passage?
It may be a verse you don't remember reading before.

3. The Wow Factor

What was the most important and impactful thing you read today? What made you say, "Wow! I'm blown away."

4. The Presence of Jesus in the Passage

What points to Jesus and His life in this passage? Does any verse remind you of something Jesus said or the way Jesus lived?

5. The Character of God

Who does God say that He is? Identify attributes from God's character in this passage. A good way to start, is to use words like: God is, God says, God does, God wants, or God can.
Review your previous answers.

6. The 'So What' or the Next Steps

Now, ask yourself, 'So what?' If what you read is true, how will you apply this? What will you do differently? What has to change?

7. Time to Pray

It is time to pray and ask God to help you. Write down your prayer to God based on what you are learning from today's passage and questions.

1. The Bible: Passage_____ and Date_____

_____/_____/_____

2. The New Thing

What is one new thing that stands out to you in today's passage?
It may be a verse you don't remember reading before.

3. The Wow Factor

What was the most important and impactful thing you read today? What made you say, "Wow! I'm blown away."

4. The Presence of Jesus in the Passage

What points to Jesus and His life in this passage? Does any verse remind you of something Jesus said or the way Jesus lived?

5. The Character of God

Who does God say that He is? Identify attributes from God's character in this passage. A good way to start, is to use words like: God is, God says, God does, God wants, or God can.
Review your previous answers.

6. The 'So What' or the Next Steps

Now, ask yourself, 'So what?' If what you read is true, how will you apply this? What will you do differently? What has to change?

7. Time to Pray

It is time to pray and ask God to help you. Write down your prayer to God based on what you are learning from today's passage and questions.

Oraciones

1. The Bible: Passage_____ and Date_____

_____/_____/_____

2. The New Thing

What is one new thing that stands out to you in today's passage?
It may be a verse you don't remember reading before.

3. The Wow Factor

What was the most important and impactful thing you read today? What made you say, "Wow! I'm blown away."

4. The Presence of Jesus in the Passage

What points to Jesus and His life in this passage? Does any verse remind you of something Jesus said or the way Jesus lived?

5. The Character of God

Who does God say that He is? Identify attributes from God's character in this passage. A good way to start, is to use words like: God is, God says, God does, God wants, or God can.
Review your previous answers.

6. The 'So What' or the Next Steps

Now, ask yourself, 'So what?' If what you read is true, how will you apply this? What will you do differently? What has to change?

7. Time to Pray

It is time to pray and ask God to help you. Write down your prayer to God based on what you are learning from today's passage and questions.

1. The Bible: Passage_____ and Date_____

_____/_____/_____

2. The New Thing

What is one new thing that stands out to you in today's passage?
It may be a verse you don't remember reading before.

3. The Wow Factor

What was the most important and impactful thing you read today? What made you say, "Wow! I'm blown away."

4. The Presence of Jesus in the Passage

What points to Jesus and His life in this passage? Does any verse remind you of something Jesus said or the way Jesus lived?

5. The Character of God

Who does God say that He is? Identify attributes from God's character in this passage. A good way to start, is to use words like: God is, God says, God does, God wants, or God can.
Review your previous answers.

6. The 'So What' or the Next Steps

Now, ask yourself, 'So what?' If what you read is true, how will you apply this? What will you do differently? What has to change?

7. Time to Pray

It is time to pray and ask God to help you. Write down your prayer to God based on what you are learning from today's passage and questions.

1. The Bible: Passage_____ and Date_____

_____/_____/_____

2. The New Thing

What is one new thing that stands out to you in today's passage?
It may be a verse you don't remember reading before.

3. The Wow Factor

What was the most important and impactful thing you read today? What made you say, "Wow! I'm blown away."

4. The Presence of Jesus in the Passage

What points to Jesus and His life in this passage? Does any verse remind you of something Jesus said or the way Jesus lived?

5. The Character of God

Who does God say that He is? Identify attributes from God's character in this passage. A good way to start, is to use words like: God is, God says, God does, God wants, or God can.
Review your previous answers.

6. The 'So What' or the Next Steps

Now, ask yourself, 'So what?' If what you read is true, how will you apply this? What will you do differently? What has to change?

7. Time to Pray

It is time to pray and ask God to help you. Write down your prayer to God based on what you are learning from today's passage and questions.

1. The Bible: Passage_____ and Date_____

_____/_____/_____

2. The New Thing

What is one new thing that stands out to you in today's passage?
It may be a verse you don't remember reading before.

3. The Wow Factor

What was the most important and impactful thing you read today? What made you say, "Wow! I'm blown away."

4. The Presence of Jesus in the Passage

What points to Jesus and His life in this passage? Does any verse remind you of something Jesus said or the way Jesus lived?

5. The Character of God

Who does God say that He is? Identify attributes from God's character in this passage. A good way to start, is to use words like: God is, God says, God does, God wants, or God can.
Review your previous answers.

6. The 'So What' or the Next Steps

Now, ask yourself, 'So what?' If what you read is true, how will you apply this? What will you do differently? What has to change?

7. Time to Pray

It is time to pray and ask God to help you. Write down your prayer to God based on what you are learning from today's passage and questions.

1. The Bible: Passage_____ and Date_____

_____/_____/_____

2. The New Thing

What is one new thing that stands out to you in today's passage?
It may be a verse you don't remember reading before.

3. The Wow Factor

What was the most important and impactful thing you read today? What made you say, "Wow! I'm
blown away."

4. The Presence of Jesus in the Passage

What points to Jesus and His life in this passage? Does any verse remind you of something Jesus said
or the way Jesus lived?

5. The Character of God

Who does God say that He is? Identify attributes from God's character in this passage. A good way to start, is to use words like: God is, God says, God does, God wants, or God can.
Review your previous answers.

6. The 'So What' or the Next Steps

Now, ask yourself, 'So what?' If what you read is true, how will you apply this? What will you do differently? What has to change?

7. Time to Pray

It is time to pray and ask God to help you. Write down your prayer to God based on what you are learning from today's passage and questions.

17 Así que la fe viene como resultado de oír el mensaje, y el mensaje que se oye es la palabra de Cristo.[a]

Romanos 10:17

Oraciones

1. The Bible: Passage_____ and Date_____

_____/_____/_____

2. The New Thing

What is one new thing that stands out to you in today's passage?
It may be a verse you don't remember reading before.

3. The Wow Factor

What was the most important and impactful thing you read today? What made you say, "Wow! I'm blown away."

4. The Presence of Jesus in the Passage

What points to Jesus and His life in this passage? Does any verse remind you of something Jesus said or the way Jesus lived?

5. The Character of God

Who does God say that He is? Identify attributes from God's character in this passage. A good way to start, is to use words like: God is, God says, God does, God wants, or God can.
Review your previous answers.

6. The 'So What' or the Next Steps

Now, ask yourself, 'So what?' If what you read is true, how will you apply this? What will you do differently? What has to change?

7. Time to Pray

It is time to pray and ask God to help you. Write down your prayer to God based on what you are learning from today's passage and questions.

1. The Bible: Passage_____ and Date_____

_____/_____/_____

2. The New Thing

What is one new thing that stands out to you in today's passage?
It may be a verse you don't remember reading before.

3. The Wow Factor

What was the most important and impactful thing you read today? What made you say, "Wow! I'm blown away."

4. The Presence of Jesus in the Passage

What points to Jesus and His life in this passage? Does any verse remind you of something Jesus said or the way Jesus lived?

5. The Character of God

Who does God say that He is? Identify attributes from God's character in this passage. A good way to start, is to use words like: God is, God says, God does, God wants, or God can.
Review your previous answers.

6. The 'So What' or the Next Steps

Now, ask yourself, 'So what?' If what you read is true, how will you apply this? What will you do differently? What has to change?

7. Time to Pray

It is time to pray and ask God to help you. Write down your prayer to God based on what you are learning from today's passage and questions.

1. The Bible: Passage_____ and Date_____

_____/_____/_____

2. The New Thing

What is one new thing that stands out to you in today's passage?
It may be a verse you don't remember reading before.

3. The Wow Factor

What was the most important and impactful thing you read today? What made you say, "Wow! I'm blown away."

4. The Presence of Jesus in the Passage

What points to Jesus and His life in this passage? Does any verse remind you of something Jesus said or the way Jesus lived?

5. The Character of God

Who does God say that He is? Identify attributes from God's character in this passage. A good way to start, is to use words like: God is, God says, God does, God wants, or God can.
Review your previous answers.

6. The 'So What' or the Next Steps

Now, ask yourself, 'So what?' If what you read is true, how will you apply this? What will you do differently? What has to change?

7. Time to Pray

It is time to pray and ask God to help you. Write down your prayer to God based on what you are learning from today's passage and questions.

1. The Bible: Passage_____ and Date_____

_____/_____/_____

2. The New Thing

What is one new thing that stands out to you in today's passage?
It may be a verse you don't remember reading before.

3. The Wow Factor

What was the most important and impactful thing you read today? What made you say, "Wow! I'm blown away."

4. The Presence of Jesus in the Passage

What points to Jesus and His life in this passage? Does any verse remind you of something Jesus said or the way Jesus lived?

5. The Character of God

Who does God say that He is? Identify attributes from God's character in this passage. A good way to start, is to use words like: God is, God says, God does, God wants, or God can.
Review your previous answers.

6. The 'So What' or the Next Steps

Now, ask yourself, 'So what?' If what you read is true, how will you apply this? What will you do differently? What has to change?

7. Time to Pray

It is time to pray and ask God to help you. Write down your prayer to God based on what you are learning from today's passage and questions.

1. The Bible: Passage_____ and Date_____

_____/_____/_____

2. The New Thing

What is one new thing that stands out to you in today's passage?
It may be a verse you don't remember reading before.

3. The Wow Factor

What was the most important and impactful thing you read today? What made you say, "Wow! I'm blown away."

4. The Presence of Jesus in the Passage

What points to Jesus and His life in this passage? Does any verse remind you of something Jesus said or the way Jesus lived?

5. The Character of God

Who does God say that He is? Identify attributes from God's character in this passage. A good way to start, is to use words like: God is, God says, God does, God wants, or God can.
Review your previous answers.

6. The 'So What' or the Next Steps

Now, ask yourself, 'So what?' If what you read is true, how will you apply this? What will you do differently? What has to change?

7. Time to Pray

It is time to pray and ask God to help you. Write down your prayer to God based on what you are learning from today's passage and questions.

Oraciones

THE 10 COMMANDMENTS
{Exodus 20:2-17 paraphrase}

1. The Bible: Passage_____ and Date_____

_____/_____/_____

2. The New Thing

What is one new thing that stands out to you in today's passage?
It may be a verse you don't remember reading before.

3. The Wow Factor

What was the most important and impactful thing you read today? What made you say, "Wow! I'm blown away."

4. The Presence of Jesus in the Passage

What points to Jesus and His life in this passage? Does any verse remind you of something Jesus said or the way Jesus lived?

5. The Character of God

Who does God say that He is? Identify attributes from God's character in this passage. A good way to start, is to use words like: God is, God says, God does, God wants, or God can.
Review your previous answers.

6. The 'So What' or the Next Steps

Now, ask yourself, 'So what?' If what you read is true, how will you apply this? What will you do differently? What has to change?

7. Time to Pray

It is time to pray and ask God to help you. Write down your prayer to God based on what you are learning from today's passage and questions.

1. The Bible: Passage_____ and Date_____

_____/_____/_____

2. The New Thing

What is one new thing that stands out to you in today's passage?
It may be a verse you don't remember reading before.

3. The Wow Factor

What was the most important and impactful thing you read today? What made you say, "Wow! I'm blown away."

4. The Presence of Jesus in the Passage

What points to Jesus and His life in this passage? Does any verse remind you of something Jesus said or the way Jesus lived?

5. The Character of God

Who does God say that He is? Identify attributes from God's character in this passage. A good way to start, is to use words like: God is, God says, God does, God wants, or God can.
Review your previous answers.

6. The 'So What' or the Next Steps

Now, ask yourself, 'So what?' If what you read is true, how will you apply this? What will you do differently? What has to change?

7. Time to Pray

It is time to pray and ask God to help you. Write down your prayer to God based on what you are learning from today's passage and questions.

1. The Bible: Passage_____ and Date_____

_____/_____/_____

2. The New Thing

What is one new thing that stands out to you in today's passage?
It may be a verse you don't remember reading before.

3. The Wow Factor

What was the most important and impactful thing you read today? What made you say, "Wow! I'm blown away."

4. The Presence of Jesus in the Passage

What points to Jesus and His life in this passage? Does any verse remind you of something Jesus said or the way Jesus lived?

5. The Character of God

Who does God say that He is? Identify attributes from God's character in this passage. A good way to start, is to use words like: God is, God says, God does, God wants, or God can.
Review your previous answers.

6. The 'So What' or the Next Steps

Now, ask yourself, 'So what?' If what you read is true, how will you apply this? What will you do differently? What has to change?

7. Time to Pray

It is time to pray and ask God to help you. Write down your prayer to God based on what you are learning from today's passage and questions.

1. The Bible: Passage_____ and Date_____

_____/_____/_____

2. The New Thing

What is one new thing that stands out to you in today's passage?
It may be a verse you don't remember reading before.

3. The Wow Factor

What was the most important and impactful thing you read today? What made you say, "Wow! I'm
blown away."

4. The Presence of Jesus in the Passage

What points to Jesus and His life in this passage? Does any verse remind you of something Jesus said
or the way Jesus lived?

5. The Character of God

Who does God say that He is? Identify attributes from God's character in this passage. A good way to start, is to use words like: God is, God says, God does, God wants, or God can.
Review your previous answers.

6. The 'So What' or the Next Steps

Now, ask yourself, 'So what?' If what you read is true, how will you apply this? What will you do differently? What has to change?

7. Time to Pray

It is time to pray and ask God to help you. Write down your prayer to God based on what you are learning from today's passage and questions.

Mateo 6:9-13

Oración del Padre

»"Padre nuestro que estás en el cielo,
santificado sea tu nombre,
[10] venga tu reino,
hágase tu voluntad
en la tierra como en el cielo.
[11] Danos hoy nuestro pan cotidiano.[a]
[12] Perdónanos nuestras deudas,
como también nosotros hemos perdonado a nuestros deudores.
[13] Y no nos dejes caer en tentación,
sino líbranos del maligno".

3 Juan 2

Oración de salud

Querido hermano, oro para que te vaya bien en
todos tus asuntos y goces de buena salud, así como
prosperas espiritualmente.

1. The Bible: Passage_____ and Date_____

_____/_____/_____

2. The New Thing

What is one new thing that stands out to you in today's passage?
It may be a verse you don't remember reading before.

3. The Wow Factor

What was the most important and impactful thing you read today? What made you say, "Wow! I'm blown away."

4. The Presence of Jesus in the Passage

What points to Jesus and His life in this passage? Does any verse remind you of something Jesus said or the way Jesus lived?

5. The Character of God

Who does God say that He is? Identify attributes from God's character in this passage. A good way to start, is to use words like: God is, God says, God does, God wants, or God can.
Review your previous answers.

6. The 'So What' or the Next Steps

Now, ask yourself, 'So what?' If what you read is true, how will you apply this? What will you do differently? What has to change?

7. Time to Pray

It is time to pray and ask God to help you. Write down your prayer to God based on what you are learning from today's passage and questions.

Sea la Luz del Mundo

Mateo 5:14

Oraciones

1. The Bible: Passage_____ and Date_____

_____/_____/_____

2. The New Thing

What is one new thing that stands out to you in today's passage?
It may be a verse you don't remember reading before.

3. The Wow Factor

What was the most important and impactful thing you read today? What made you say, "Wow! I'm blown away."

4. The Presence of Jesus in the Passage

What points to Jesus and His life in this passage? Does any verse remind you of something Jesus said or the way Jesus lived?

5. The Character of God

Who does God say that He is? Identify attributes from God's character in this passage. A good way to start, is to use words like: God is, God says, God does, God wants, or God can.
Review your previous answers.

6. The 'So What' or the Next Steps

Now, ask yourself, 'So what?' If what you read is true, how will you apply this? What will you do differently? What has to change?

7. Time to Pray

It is time to pray and ask God to help you. Write down your prayer to God based on what you are learning from today's passage and questions.

1. The Bible: Passage_____ and Date_____

_____/_____/_____

2. The New Thing

What is one new thing that stands out to you in today's passage?
It may be a verse you don't remember reading before.

3. The Wow Factor

What was the most important and impactful thing you read today? What made you say, "Wow! I'm blown away."

4. The Presence of Jesus in the Passage

What points to Jesus and His life in this passage? Does any verse remind you of something Jesus said or the way Jesus lived?

5. The Character of God

Who does God say that He is? Identify attributes from God's character in this passage. A good way to start, is to use words like: God is, God says, God does, God wants, or God can.
Review your previous answers.

6. The 'So What' or the Next Steps

Now, ask yourself, 'So what?' If what you read is true, how will you apply this? What will you do differently? What has to change?

7. Time to Pray

It is time to pray and ask God to help you. Write down your prayer to God based on what you are learning from today's passage and questions.

1. The Bible: Passage_____ and Date_____

_____/_____/_____

2. The New Thing

What is one new thing that stands out to you in today's passage?
It may be a verse you don't remember reading before.

3. The Wow Factor

What was the most important and impactful thing you read today? What made you say, "Wow! I'm blown away."

4. The Presence of Jesus in the Passage

What points to Jesus and His life in this passage? Does any verse remind you of something Jesus said or the way Jesus lived?

5. The Character of God

Who does God say that He is? Identify attributes from God's character in this passage. A good way to start, is to use words like: God is, God says, God does, God wants, or God can.
Review your previous answers.

6. The 'So What' or the Next Steps

Now, ask yourself, 'So what?' If what you read is true, how will you apply this? What will you do differently? What has to change?

7. Time to Pray

It is time to pray and ask God to help you. Write down your prayer to God based on what you are learning from today's passage and questions.

1. The Bible: Passage_____ and Date_____

_____/_____/_____

2. The New Thing

What is one new thing that stands out to you in today's passage?
It may be a verse you don't remember reading before.

3. The Wow Factor

What was the most important and impactful thing you read today? What made you say, "Wow! I'm blown away."

4. The Presence of Jesus in the Passage

What points to Jesus and His life in this passage? Does any verse remind you of something Jesus said or the way Jesus lived?

5. The Character of God

Who does God say that He is? Identify attributes from God's character in this passage. A good way to start, is to use words like: God is, God says, God does, God wants, or God can.
Review your previous answers.

6. The 'So What' or the Next Steps

Now, ask yourself, 'So what?' If what you read is true, how will you apply this? What will you do differently? What has to change?

7. Time to Pray

It is time to pray and ask God to help you. Write down your prayer to God based on what you are learning from today's passage and questions.

1. The Bible: Passage_____ and Date_____

_____/_____/_____

2. The New Thing

What is one new thing that stands out to you in today's passage?
It may be a verse you don't remember reading before.

3. The Wow Factor

What was the most important and impactful thing you read today? What made you say, "Wow! I'm blown away."

4. The Presence of Jesus in the Passage

What points to Jesus and His life in this passage? Does any verse remind you of something Jesus said or the way Jesus lived?

5. The Character of God

Who does God say that He is? Identify attributes from God's character in this passage. A good way to start, is to use words like: God is, God says, God does, God wants, or God can.
Review your previous answers.

6. The 'So What' or the Next Steps

Now, ask yourself, 'So what?' If what you read is true, how will you apply this? What will you do differently? What has to change?

7. Time to Pray

It is time to pray and ask God to help you. Write down your prayer to God based on what you are learning from today's passage and questions.

Oraciones

³² y conocerán la verdad, y la verdad los hará libres.

Juan 8:32

1. The Bible: Passage_____ and Date_____

_____/_____/_____

2. The New Thing

What is one new thing that stands out to you in today's passage?
It may be a verse you don't remember reading before.

3. The Wow Factor

What was the most important and impactful thing you read today? What made you say, "Wow! I'm blown away."

4. The Presence of Jesus in the Passage

What points to Jesus and His life in this passage? Does any verse remind you of something Jesus said or the way Jesus lived?

5. The Character of God

Who does God say that He is? Identify attributes from God's character in this passage. A good way to start, is to use words like: God is, God says, God does, God wants, or God can.
Review your previous answers.

6. The 'So What' or the Next Steps

Now, ask yourself, 'So what?' If what you read is true, how will you apply this? What will you do differently? What has to change?

7. Time to Pray

It is time to pray and ask God to help you. Write down your prayer to God based on what you are learning from today's passage and questions.

1. The Bible: Passage_____ and Date_____

_____/_____/_____

2. The New Thing

What is one new thing that stands out to you in today's passage?
It may be a verse you don't remember reading before.

3. The Wow Factor

What was the most important and impactful thing you read today? What made you say, "Wow! I'm blown away."

4. The Presence of Jesus in the Passage

What points to Jesus and His life in this passage? Does any verse remind you of something Jesus said or the way Jesus lived?

5. The Character of God

Who does God say that He is? Identify attributes from God's character in this passage. A good way to start, is to use words like: God is, God says, God does, God wants, or God can.
Review your previous answers.

6. The 'So What' or the Next Steps

Now, ask yourself, 'So what?' If what you read is true, how will you apply this? What will you do differently? What has to change?

7. Time to Pray

It is time to pray and ask God to help you. Write down your prayer to God based on what you are learning from today's passage and questions.

Oración de Jonás

² Entonces Jonás oró al SEÑOR su Dios desde el vientre del pez. ² Dijo:

«En mi angustia clamé al SEÑOR,

y él me respondió.

Desde las entrañas del sepulcro pedí auxilio,

y tú escuchaste mi clamor.

³ A lo profundo me arrojaste,

al corazón mismo de los mares;

las corrientes me envolvían,

todas tus ondas y tus olas pasaban sobre mí.

⁴ Y pensé: "He sido expulsado

de tu presencia.

¿Cómo volveré a contemplar

tu santo templo?"

⁵ Las aguas me llegaban hasta el cuello,

lo profundo del océano me envolvía;

las algas se me enredaban en la cabeza,

6   arrastrándome a los cimientos de las montañas.

Me tragó la tierra, y para siempre

sus cerrojos se cerraron tras de mí.

Pero tú, SEÑOR, Dios mío,

me rescataste de la fosa.

7 »Al sentir que se me iba la vida,

me acordé del SEÑOR,

y mi oración llegó hasta ti,

hasta tu santo templo.

8 »Los que siguen a ídolos vanos

abandonan el amor de Dios.

9 Yo, en cambio, te ofreceré sacrificios

y cánticos de gratitud.

Cumpliré las promesas que te hice.

¡La salvación viene del SEÑOR!»

1. The Bible: Passage_____ and Date_____

_____/_____/_____

2. The New Thing

What is one new thing that stands out to you in today's passage?
It may be a verse you don't remember reading before.

3. The Wow Factor

What was the most important and impactful thing you read today? What made you say, "Wow! I'm blown away."

4. The Presence of Jesus in the Passage

What points to Jesus and His life in this passage? Does any verse remind you of something Jesus said or the way Jesus lived?

5. The Character of God

Who does God say that He is? Identify attributes from God's character in this passage. A good way to start, is to use words like: God is, God says, God does, God wants, or God can.
Review your previous answers.

6. The 'So What' or the Next Steps

Now, ask yourself, 'So what?' If what you read is true, how will you apply this? What will you do differently? What has to change?

7. Time to Pray

It is time to pray and ask God to help you. Write down your prayer to God based on what you are learning from today's passage and questions.

1. The Bible: Passage_____ and Date_____

_____/_____/_____

2. The New Thing

What is one new thing that stands out to you in today's passage?
It may be a verse you don't remember reading before.

3. The Wow Factor

What was the most important and impactful thing you read today? What made you say, "Wow! I'm blown away."

4. The Presence of Jesus in the Passage

What points to Jesus and His life in this passage? Does any verse remind you of something Jesus said or the way Jesus lived?

5. The Character of God

Who does God say that He is? Identify attributes from God's character in this passage. A good way to start, is to use words like: God is, God says, God does, God wants, or God can.
Review your previous answers.

6. The 'So What' or the Next Steps

Now, ask yourself, 'So what?' If what you read is true, how will you apply this? What will you do differently? What has to change?

7. Time to Pray

It is time to pray and ask God to help you. Write down your prayer to God based on what you are learning from today's passage and questions.

1. The Bible: Passage_____ and Date_____

_____/_____/_____

2. The New Thing

What is one new thing that stands out to you in today's passage?
It may be a verse you don't remember reading before.

3. The Wow Factor

What was the most important and impactful thing you read today? What made you say, "Wow! I'm blown away."

4. The Presence of Jesus in the Passage

What points to Jesus and His life in this passage? Does any verse remind you of something Jesus said or the way Jesus lived?

5. The Character of God

Who does God say that He is? Identify attributes from God's character in this passage. A good way to start, is to use words like: God is, God says, God does, God wants, or God can.
Review your previous answers.

6. The 'So What' or the Next Steps

Now, ask yourself, 'So what?' If what you read is true, how will you apply this? What will you do differently? What has to change?

7. Time to Pray

It is time to pray and ask God to help you. Write down your prayer to God based on what you are learning from today's passage and questions.

⁴ Jesús le respondió:
—Escrito está: "No solo de pan vive el hombre, sino de toda palabra que sale de la boca de Dios".

Mateo 4:4

DE LA Abundancia
LUCAS 6:45
Corazón
habla su boca.

Oraciones

1. The Bible: Passage_____ and Date_____

_____/_____/_____

2. The New Thing

What is one new thing that stands out to you in today's passage?
It may be a verse you don't remember reading before.

3. The Wow Factor

What was the most important and impactful thing you read today? What made you say, "Wow! I'm blown away."

4. The Presence of Jesus in the Passage

What points to Jesus and His life in this passage? Does any verse remind you of something Jesus said or the way Jesus lived?

5. The Character of God

Who does God say that He is? Identify attributes from God's character in this passage. A good way to start, is to use words like: God is, God says, God does, God wants, or God can.
Review your previous answers.

6. The 'So What' or the Next Steps

Now, ask yourself, 'So what?' If what you read is true, how will you apply this? What will you do differently? What has to change?

7. Time to Pray

It is time to pray and ask God to help you. Write down your prayer to God based on what you are learning from today's passage and questions.

1. The Bible: Passage_____ and Date_____

_____/_____/_____

2. The New Thing

What is one new thing that stands out to you in today's passage?
It may be a verse you don't remember reading before.

3. The Wow Factor

What was the most important and impactful thing you read today? What made you say, "Wow! I'm blown away."

4. The Presence of Jesus in the Passage

What points to Jesus and His life in this passage? Does any verse remind you of something Jesus said or the way Jesus lived?

5. The Character of God

Who does God say that He is? Identify attributes from God's character in this passage. A good way to start, is to use words like: God is, God says, God does, God wants, or God can.
Review your previous answers.

6. The 'So What' or the Next Steps

Now, ask yourself, 'So what?' If what you read is true, how will you apply this? What will you do differently? What has to change?

7. Time to Pray

It is time to pray and ask God to help you. Write down your prayer to God based on what you are learning from today's passage and questions.

1. The Bible: Passage_____ and Date_____

_____/_____/_____

2. The New Thing

What is one new thing that stands out to you in today's passage?
It may be a verse you don't remember reading before.

3. The Wow Factor

What was the most important and impactful thing you read today? What made you say, "Wow! I'm blown away."

4. The Presence of Jesus in the Passage

What points to Jesus and His life in this passage? Does any verse remind you of something Jesus said or the way Jesus lived?

5. The Character of God

Who does God say that He is? Identify attributes from God's character in this passage. A good way to start, is to use words like: God is, God says, God does, God wants, or God can.
Review your previous answers.

6. The 'So What' or the Next Steps

Now, ask yourself, 'So what?' If what you read is true, how will you apply this? What will you do differently? What has to change?

7. Time to Pray

It is time to pray and ask God to help you. Write down your prayer to God based on what you are learning from today's passage and questions.

1. The Bible: Passage_____ and Date_____

_____/_____/_____

2. The New Thing

What is one new thing that stands out to you in today's passage?
It may be a verse you don't remember reading before.

3. The Wow Factor

What was the most important and impactful thing you read today? What made you say, "Wow! I'm blown away."

4. The Presence of Jesus in the Passage

What points to Jesus and His life in this passage? Does any verse remind you of something Jesus said or the way Jesus lived?

5. The Character of God

Who does God say that He is? Identify attributes from God's character in this passage. A good way to start, is to use words like: God is, God says, God does, God wants, or God can.
Review your previous answers.

6. The 'So What' or the Next Steps

Now, ask yourself, 'So what?' If what you read is true, how will you apply this? What will you do differently? What has to change?

7. Time to Pray

It is time to pray and ask God to help you. Write down your prayer to God based on what you are learning from today's passage and questions.

Oración para sabiduría

Me dije a mí mismo:

«Mientras esté ante gente malvada

vigilaré mi conducta,

me abstendré de pecar con la lengua,

me pondré una mordaza en la boca».

² Así que guardé silencio, me mantuve callado.

¡Ni aun lo bueno salía de mi boca!

Pero mi angustia iba en aumento;

³ ¡el corazón me ardía en el pecho!

Al meditar en esto, el fuego se inflamó

y tuve que decir:

⁴ «Hazme saber, SEÑOR, el límite de mis días,

y el tiempo que me queda por vivir;

hazme saber lo efímero que soy.

⁵ Muy breve es la vida que me has dado;

ante ti, mis años no son nada.

¡Un soplo nada más es el mortal! Selah

⁶ Es un suspiro que se pierde entre las sombras.

Ilusorias son las riquezas que amontona,

pues no sabe quién se quedará con ellas.

7 »Y ahora, Señor, ¿qué esperanza me queda?

¡Mi esperanza he puesto en ti!

8 Líbrame de todas mis transgresiones.

Que los necios no se burlen de mí.

9 »He guardado silencio; no he abierto la boca,

pues tú eres quien actúa.

10 Ya no me castigues,

que los golpes de tu mano me aniquilan.

11 Tú reprendes a los mortales,

los castigas por su iniquidad;

como polilla, acabas con sus placeres.

¡Un soplo nada más es el mortal! Selah

12 »SEÑOR, escucha mi oración,

atiende a mi clamor;

no cierres tus oídos a mi llanto.

Ante ti soy un extraño,

un peregrino, como todos mis antepasados.

13 No me mires con enojo, y volveré a alegrarme

antes que me muera y deje de existir».

1. The Bible: Passage_____ and Date_____

_____/_____/_____

2. The New Thing

What is one new thing that stands out to you in today's passage?
It may be a verse you don't remember reading before.

3. The Wow Factor

What was the most important and impactful thing you read today? What made you say, "Wow! I'm
blown away."

4. The Presence of Jesus in the Passage

What points to Jesus and His life in this passage? Does any verse remind you of something Jesus said
or the way Jesus lived?

5. The Character of God

Who does God say that He is? Identify attributes from God's character in this passage. A good way to start, is to use words like: God is, God says, God does, God wants, or God can.
Review your previous answers.

6. The 'So What' or the Next Steps

Now, ask yourself, 'So what?' If what you read is true, how will you apply this? What will you do differently? What has to change?

7. Time to Pray

It is time to pray and ask God to help you. Write down your prayer to God based on what you are learning from today's passage and questions.

Oraciones

¹² No me he apartado de los mandamientos de sus labios;
en lo más profundo de mi ser[a]
he atesorado las palabras de su boca.

Job 23:12

tus OJOS
Vieron mi
SALMO 139:16
Embrion

1. The Bible: Passage_____ and Date_____

_____/_____/_____

2. The New Thing

What is one new thing that stands out to you in today's passage?
It may be a verse you don't remember reading before.

3. The Wow Factor

What was the most important and impactful thing you read today? What made you say, "Wow! I'm blown away."

4. The Presence of Jesus in the Passage

What points to Jesus and His life in this passage? Does any verse remind you of something Jesus said or the way Jesus lived?

5. The Character of God

Who does God say that He is? Identify attributes from God's character in this passage. A good way to start, is to use words like: God is, God says, God does, God wants, or God can.
Review your previous answers.

6. The 'So What' or the Next Steps

Now, ask yourself, 'So what?' If what you read is true, how will you apply this? What will you do differently? What has to change?

7. Time to Pray

It is time to pray and ask God to help you. Write down your prayer to God based on what you are learning from today's passage and questions.

1. The Bible: Passage_____ and Date_____

_____/_____/_____

2. The New Thing

What is one new thing that stands out to you in today's passage?
It may be a verse you don't remember reading before.

3. The Wow Factor

What was the most important and impactful thing you read today? What made you say, "Wow! I'm blown away."

4. The Presence of Jesus in the Passage

What points to Jesus and His life in this passage? Does any verse remind you of something Jesus said or the way Jesus lived?

5. The Character of God

Who does God say that He is? Identify attributes from God's character in this passage. A good way to start, is to use words like: God is, God says, God does, God wants, or God can.
Review your previous answers.

6. The 'So What' or the Next Steps

Now, ask yourself, 'So what?' If what you read is true, how will you apply this? What will you do differently? What has to change?

7. Time to Pray

It is time to pray and ask God to help you. Write down your prayer to God based on what you are learning from today's passage and questions.

1. The Bible: Passage_____ and Date_____

_____/_____/_____

2. The New Thing

What is one new thing that stands out to you in today's passage?
It may be a verse you don't remember reading before.

3. The Wow Factor

What was the most important and impactful thing you read today? What made you say, "Wow! I'm blown away."

4. The Presence of Jesus in the Passage

What points to Jesus and His life in this passage? Does any verse remind you of something Jesus said or the way Jesus lived?

5. The Character of God

Who does God say that He is? Identify attributes from God's character in this passage. A good way to start, is to use words like: God is, God says, God does, God wants, or God can.
Review your previous answers.

6. The 'So What' or the Next Steps

Now, ask yourself, 'So what?' If what you read is true, how will you apply this? What will you do differently? What has to change?

7. Time to Pray

It is time to pray and ask God to help you. Write down your prayer to God based on what you are learning from today's passage and questions.

1. The Bible: Passage_____ and Date_____

_____/_____/_____

2. The New Thing

What is one new thing that stands out to you in today's passage?
It may be a verse you don't remember reading before.

3. The Wow Factor

What was the most important and impactful thing you read today? What made you say, "Wow! I'm blown away."

4. The Presence of Jesus in the Passage

What points to Jesus and His life in this passage? Does any verse remind you of something Jesus said or the way Jesus lived?

5. The Character of God

Who does God say that He is? Identify attributes from God's character in this passage. A good way to start, is to use words like: God is, God says, God does, God wants, or God can.
Review your previous answers.

6. The 'So What' or the Next Steps

Now, ask yourself, 'So what?' If what you read is true, how will you apply this? What will you do differently? What has to change?

7. Time to Pray

It is time to pray and ask God to help you. Write down your prayer to God based on what you are learning from today's passage and questions.

1. The Bible: Passage_____ and Date_____

_____/_____/_____

2. The New Thing

What is one new thing that stands out to you in today's passage?
It may be a verse you don't remember reading before.

3. The Wow Factor

What was the most important and impactful thing you read today? What made you say, "Wow! I'm blown away."

4. The Presence of Jesus in the Passage

What points to Jesus and His life in this passage? Does any verse remind you of something Jesus said or the way Jesus lived?

5. The Character of God

Who does God say that He is? Identify attributes from God's character in this passage. A good way to start, is to use words like: God is, God says, God does, God wants, or God can.
Review your previous answers.

6. The 'So What' or the Next Steps

Now, ask yourself, 'So what?' If what you read is true, how will you apply this? What will you do differently? What has to change?

7. Time to Pray

It is time to pray and ask God to help you. Write down your prayer to God based on what you are learning from today's passage and questions.

³⁵ **El cielo y la tierra pasarán, pero mis palabras jamás pasarán.**

Mateo 24:35

Oraciones

Notas

Notas

Sea la Luz del Mundo

Mateo 5:14

Notas

SEA LA Luz del Mundo

Mateo 5:14

Notas

Mateo 5:14

Notas

Notas

Sea la Luz del Mundo

Mateo 5:14

Notas

Notas

Notas

Sea la Luz del Mundo

Mateo 5:14

Notas

Sea la Luz del Mundo

Mateo 5:14

Notas

Sea la Luz del Mundo

Mateo 5:14

DEVOTIONAL
PRAYER BOOK
FOR
Women

100 DAYS EXPERIENCING GOD
THROUGH A 7-STEP DAILY BIBLE STUDY

DEVOTIONAL PRAYER JOURNALS

SCAN ME

to get all the books